A Handbook for the
Study of Poetry

A
HANDBOOK FOR THE
STUDY OF POETRY

by

LYNN ALTENBERND
University of Illinois

and

LESLIE L. LEWIS
University of Colorado

The Macmillan Company, New York
Collier-Macmillan Limited, London

ACKNOWLEDGMENT

The poem "How Annandale Went Out" is reprinted with the permission of Charles Scribner's Sons, from *The Town Down the River* by Edwin Arlington Robinson. Copyright 1910 by Charles Scribner's Sons; renewal copyright 1938 by Ruth Nivison.

© COPYRIGHT, THE MACMILLAN COMPANY, 1966

SECOND PRINTING, 1966

This book is a revised and expanded version of part one of *Introduction to Literature: Poems* by Lynn Altenbernd and Leslie L. Lewis, © copyright 1963 by The Macmillan Company.

Library of Congress catalog card number: 66–14198

The Macmillan Company, New York
Collier-Macmillan Canada, Ltd., Toronto, Ontario

Printed in the United States of America

Introduction

The three little books called A *Handbook for the Study of Fiction*, A *Handbook for the Study of Poetry*, and A *Handbook for the Study of Drama* are revisions and enlargements of the handbook sections in our *Introduction to Literature: Stories, Poems, Plays*. In their present form the handbooks are intended for use with editions of individual works or with any anthology that lacks similar instructional materials. These books are intended to facilitate rather than to forestall classroom discussion—hence, they set forth their principles briefly, without elaboration, and with modest amounts of illustration. The authors have concentrated on preliminary and elementary suggestions for reading literary works. Thus the student with little earlier experience in these matters may find help in getting started, whereas the more advanced student should find the handbooks useful for review. Often the teacher may wish to develop points beyond our discussion of them or, if the class procedure is inductive, to use the handbooks as references that succinctly summarize the discussion. Of course, they are no substitute for the guidance of an intelligent and sympathetic teacher.

Extensive reading of many kinds of poetry—that one indispensable activity for the study of the type—can proceed along with the study of aspects of poetry. Initially the student may be able to appreciate only the more obvious merits of the poems he reads and to give only the most rudimentary account of the sources of his enjoyment. Hence, many poems will have to be left before they have been satisfactorily treated. The acquisition of understanding is cumulative, though, and the student will move by imperceptible stages toward what will appear to be the intuitive apprehension of the whole poem.

Urbana, Illinois   L.A.
Boulder, Colorado   L.L.L.

Contents

IV. THE CONTENT OF POETRY—Continued

A Handbook for the
Study of Poetry

I

The Nature of Poetry

Poetry has been produced by every civilization in history, and it shows no sign of losing its power in our time. Ours may be, as we are often told, a prosaic age or a scientific age, but it is also an age in which a great quantity of poetry is written. It may ultimately prove to be one of the great eras of poetic creation. The remarkable durability of the poetic tradition and the intensification of poetic composition in times of critical transition—the Renaissance and the twentieth century—indicate that poetry is closely related to mankind's deepest concerns. It not only records and comments on events, but also helps to define our responses to them. If its special province is emotion, it is nevertheless also admirably suited to handling narrative or ideas.

One source of poetry's viability is its remarkable power to adapt to changing circumstances. As it once celebrated the astonishing oceangoing vessels of the fifteenth century, so it has now assimilated airplanes and rockets. But poetry can accommodate itself to new ways of living because it is also an expression of the unchanging and universal essence of human experience.

One result of poetry's constant stretching and shifting to cover the elastic shape of life is the appearance of new

1

forms of expression without loss of the old ones. Gerard Manley Hopkins, E. E. Cummings, Dylan Thomas, and many more have startlingly reshaped the language of poetry without preventing anyone else from writing in traditional verse patterns. Still the nature of poetry is unchanged by its growing diversity of forms. We may still define it as the *interpretive dramatization of experience in metrical language.*

Poetry shares many qualities with other forms of writing, but it also has many distinctive characteristics. Here is a well-known poem that will give us an opportunity at the outset to observe both the similarities and differences between poetry and other writing, and to consider some of the initial difficulties peculiar to poetry:

Ozymandias

I met a traveller from an antique land
Who said: Two vast and trunkless legs of stone
Stand in the desert . . . Near them, on the sand,
Half sunk, a shattered visage lies, whose frown,
And wrinkled lip, and sneer of cold command,
Tell that its sculptor well those passions read
Which yet survive, stamped on these lifeless things,
The hand that mocked them, and the heart that fed:
And on the pedestal these words appear:
"My name is Ozymandias, king of kings: 10
Look on my works, ye Mighty, and despair!"
Nothing beside remains. Round the decay
Of that colossal wreck, boundless and bare
The lone and level sands stretch far away.

Obviously we must know the meaning of each word; sometimes we shall have to use the dictionary to look up unfamiliar words or to discover an unusual sense of a familiar one, but more often the situation in the poem itself will sufficiently indicate the dictionary meaning of any word we are unsure of. Here probably only the proper name, Ozymandias, will be unfamiliar, and the poem tells us all we need to know about him. Ozymandias was an actual king of Egypt; his statue was described by a Greek historian, but it had disappeared by Shelley's time. In this instance such additional information adds little to our understanding of the poem, but in other situations it might be essential. Some of Edwin Arlington Robinson's poems, addressed to writers of the past, mean very little to a reader who does not recognize the name of George Crabbe or Max Nordau. Some of the words in the poem are somewhat unexpected synonyms for common terms. What is the effect, for example, of the poet's using "antique" instead of "ancient"? The difference in the normal accenting of the two words is not significant, for the rhythm of the line would be irregular with either alternative. The word "antique" suggests not only that the unidentified land was very old, but also that it was somewhat quaint and outmoded—qualities that prepare us for the loss of grandeur by a once great king. In the fourth line the term "visage" is a formal synonym for "face," so that it contributes to the picture of a haughty commander.

"Ozymandias," like most poems, is written in normal English sentences. Our first concern is to understand the *plain sense* of these sentences, using the poet's punctuation and our own knowledge of grammar and sentence structure as guides. Sometimes, though, the compression and condensation of poetry make a sentence obscure. In such instances, we should do well to identify the grammatical relationships of the sentence parts as an aid to understanding and as a guide to effective oral reading. In "Ozymandias" line eight presents a difficulty: how are these phrases related to the rest of the sentence? The hand of the sculptor mocked—in the sense that it both imitated and derided—the passions of the king, and the heart of the king himself fed those passions. But the line seems to dangle unless we realize that "survive" means "outlive" the hand and the heart, which are objects of the verb even though they are separated from it by the phrase "stamped on these lifeless things." "Stamped on these lifeless things" modifies "passions."

Poetry differs from some kinds of prose in usually being more *concrete* and *specific*. That is, it communicates experiences, emotions, attitudes, and propositions by dealing with a particular situation or event that implicitly embodies abstract generalizations. In "Ozymandias" Shelley presents a desert scene from which we can deduce the fall of a proud kingdom. He need not state the "lesson" of this scene because the physical objects clearly embody the idea that human vanity comes to naught. Poets do sometimes state the abstract principles demonstrated in their work, but we usually conclude that abstract statement fails when it is not thoroughly incorporated in concrete and specific *dramatic symbols*. Like other literature, poetry uses a *dramatic method* in the sense that it acts out whatever ideas it conveys.

Poetry often uses an imagined *dramatic situation* which can be defined by the answers to some or all of these questions: Who is speaking? To whom? Under what circumstances? What is the speaker's attitude toward the subject of his discourse? Toward his audience? Sometimes quotation marks indicate that the poem consists of the words of a fictional speaker, but their absence does not mean that the poet has not imagined a character who speaks the lines. "Ozymandias" describes its dramatic situation more overtly than most poems do. The sequence of two narrators (the "I," who speaks first, and the "traveller from an antique land") stresses the remoteness of the scene from contemporary life and augments the reader's sense of the long lapse of the centuries.

Poetry usually includes some element of *narrative*; this story, overt or implied, may be the matter of chief interest in the poem, or it may be the means of conveying an attitude or a proposition. The important narrative element of "Ozymandias" is implied, as we have seen, but it is of central importance in the poem, and the more impressive because the reader reconstructs it.

Poetry communicates in many ways at once. The several means of communication interact with each other—

and may reinforce, qualify, or counteract each other—to produce a net effect which is greater than the impact of the several components taken separately. Our example has shown how the sentence structure, the concreteness of detail, the meanings and associations of words, and the implied dramatic situation all contribute to the total effect of the poem. A work of art must be experienced as a whole; it is not merely a theme carted along in a vehicle, but an inseparable fusion—a complete flowing together—of theme and form. Consider the following brief poem by Robert Browning:

Meeting at Night

The grey sea and the long black land;
And the yellow half-moon large and low;
And the startled little waves that leap
In fiery ringlets from their sleep,
As I gain the cove with pushing prow,
And quench its speed i' the slushy sand.

Then a mile of warm sea-scented beach;
Three fields to cross till a farm appears;
A tap at the pane, the quick sharp scratch
And blue spurt of a lighted match,   10
And a voice less loud, thro' its joys and fears,
Than the two hearts beating each to each!

The narrative content of this poem is slim indeed. The slender story is implied rather than stated, for the poet has used no complete sentence in either stanza. In addition, to say that the poem embodies the emotions of a lover hastening to a nighttime tryst is to drain it of all the vividly realized experience that can be conveyed only by the whole poem. The images of the opening lines are rather general in order to suggest that only the vague outlines of sea and land are visible in the darkness. The colors are similarly muted. Indeed, because the scene does not provide precise and brilliant visual images, the poet appeals to the several other senses that become more alert

when eyesight does not serve. The sixth line with its sequence of *s* sounds (including the variants *ch* and *sh*)
suggests the hushed noise of the boat nosing into the
beach. In the seventh line the glow of heat remaining in
the sand and the smell of the seashore appeal to other
senses. In the ninth line the series of short, rapid syllables
in "A tap at the pane" and the slower, longer, accented
syllables of "the quick sharp scratch" aptly imitate the
sounds named in the phrases. The tenth line contains one
final vivid but brief visual image. The effect of the images
is to make the reader live through the experience rather
than merely hear about it.

Browning has also deftly manipulated rhythms and
combined them with consonant and vowel sounds to suggest the tempo of the action and emotional quickening or
relaxation. The basic meter is iambic tetrameter; that is,
the normal line would have eight syllables alternately unaccented and accented. Few of the lines are perfectly regular and several kinds of variations appear. The normal
line is smooth, easy, and moderately slow in movement,
but the conversion of one or more normally unaccented
syllables to accents slows the pace. Thus in the first line
"grey," "sea," "long," "black," and "land" are all accented;
the line is slowed down and lengthened so that it suggests prolonged gliding over a calm sea. The second line
is regular except for the addition of an unaccented syllable
at the beginning; its movement is similarly moderate. The
effect of the rhythm is strengthened by the frequent occurrence of *l* sounds which are prolonged in oral reading. In
the third line the *l*'s alternate with *t*'s to produce the
choppy effect of wavelets near the shore. In the last two
lines the movement is quickened by the addition of unaccented syllables, which, though they add to the total of
syllables in the line, must be pronounced rapidly and
hence hasten the movement. Thus "And a," "thro' its,"
and "Than the" all speed up the lines to suggest quickening of the pulse at the moment of encounter. In the last
line "two," "hearts," and "beat-" are all accented (al-

though "hearts" has a light accent) to slow down the pace and prepare for reassurance and repose as the poem concludes on two regular iambic measures like heartbeats.

This prose commentary, already much longer than the poem itself, is certainly no fair substitute for it. Our analysis is far from exhaustive, and it arbitrarily separates elements that in the poem work together to produce the total effect. The remainder of our discussion will consider in more detail how these elements and others are fused to produce the whole poem.

II

The Language of Poetry

The selection of words in a poem is called its *diction*. Because poetry is compressed and intense, and because it communicates in many ways at once, the poet chooses his words with great care. The reader, therefore, must be alert to the precise meaning and implication in the diction of a poem. This is not to say that there is a special vocabulary appropriate to poetry only. The notion that contractions like "o'er" or archaisms like "ere" make pedestrian writing soar on the wings of Pegasus was never valid, and the use of fancy epithets like "finny tribe" when the poet meant "fish" went out of fashion nearly two hundred years ago. The poet chooses the words most appropriate to his purpose in a given poem, and since the whole range of human activities, ideas, and emotions is now within the province of poetry, the entire vocabulary of the language may be sifted for the right words.

A. Diction: Denotation and Connotation

Two aspects of a word may usefully be distinguished: *denotation* and *connotation*.

The *denotation* of a word is its dictionary definition—

the thing that the word names, describes, or narrates, presumably considered in a detached, scientific, and descriptive (rather than evaluative) manner. We must be sure, of course, that we understand the correct dictionary meaning of each word. These lines from the "The Rubáiyát of Omar Kháyyám" show an unusual denotation of the word "gin":

> O Thou, who didst with Pitfall and with Gin
> Beset the Road I was to wander in, . . .

Because Omar praises wine, we might be led to suppose that he refers here to hard drink as one of the hazards of his life. Another denotation of "gin," though, is a trap set across a path to catch game. This meaning of the word harmonizes with "pitfall" and "road," and produces a more precise and consistent picture. Similarly, the second line of Edwin Arlington Robinson's "Credo" contains an unexpected word:

> I cannot find my way: there is no star
> In all the shrouded heavens anywhere; . . .

The sound values of the line would be nearly the same if the poet had written "clouded," and the statement would be literally accurate. "Shrouded" means wrapped in a shroud, a burial garment. Thus the denotation of the word figuratively pictures the skies as a once living entity now dead.

In addition, "shrouded" carries with it associations of death, corpses, mourning, and muteness; it imparts an uneasy sense of horror and loathing. This accumulation of emotional associations that a word has gathered through its history or acquires in a given setting is called its *connotation*. Connotation supplements denotation by indicating attitudes and values, by fleshing out the bare bones of meaning with flavor or wit. Consider the differences of connotation in these pairs of words which are essentially synonymous in denotation: house-home; dog-cur; girl-wench; face-visage; report-rumor; damage-mischief; conciliate-appease; mundane-worldly; enmity-hostility; pride-vanity; tremble-shudder; adventurous-daring; disciple-henchman. In each instance some shift in denotation is involved, but the difference in connotation is much more striking. Usually the poet communicates through widely shared connotations, but sometimes he uses limited or even personal connotations that may be discovered by a study of his times, his life, or his other works. The reader, too, may bring personal connotations to the reading of a poem, as some people have learned to love snakes and to loathe puppies. These contributions may enrich the poem, but they are more likely to obscure it.

Both denotations and public connotations may change over the years. Usually we benefit from knowing at least the approximate date of the poem, so that we may understand each word in the sense the poet intended. In "The Rime of the Ancient Mariner," the old sailor speaks of "the *silly* buckets on the deck." Here the word "silly" means "simple" or "rustic," an archaic sense of the term which Coleridge uses to add to the ghostly antiquity of his narrator. In the Renaissance, the word also meant "frail," "helpless," or "innocent," so that we encounter the phrase "silly sheep." Applying our modern denotation of "foolish" or "stupid" would prevent our understanding the lines. Literature tends to fix connotations and to give them wide currency; nevertheless shifting connotations also may present difficulties. In his "Ode to Autumn," Keats refers to the cells of a honeycomb as "clammy." In current usage this word, especially in the pat phrase, "cold and clammy," suggests something damp, chilly, and repulsive. The dictionary defines the term as "soft, moist, and sticky," so that the denotation of the word is perfectly appropriate if we disregard the popular connotations it has acquired.

B. Imagery

Another quality of language especially important in poetry is its power to produce in the mind an effect very nearly the same as that created by stimulation of the sensory organs. We sometimes speak of mental pictures; we mean an effect in the mind much like that produced by our perceiving a visible object through the eye, the optic nerve, and the appropriate regions of the brain. Consider the following stanza from "The Eve of St. Agnes":

> A casement high and triple-arched there was,
> All garland with carven imag'ries
> Of fruits, and flowers, and bunches of knot-grass,
> And diamonded with panes of quaint device,
> Innumerable of stains and splendid dyes,
> As are the tiger-moth's deep-damasked wings;
> And in the midst, 'mong thousand heraldries,
> And twilight saints, and dim emblazonings,
>   A shielded scutcheon blushed with blood of
>   queens and kings.

Keats names and describes a number of visible objects: A "casement" (why not a "window"?) is "high" and "triple-arched"; it is "garlanded" with carvings of fruit, flowers, and bunches of knot-grass; diamond-shaped panes of stained glass show the colors of the tiger moth's wing; and so through the stanza. These mental pictures and the language that presents them are called *imagery*; the individual pictures (or the words embodying them) are called *images*.

Once again we must understand the meanings of the words, which in this connection probably also means that we must be able to recall a sense experience of the objects named and described, or imaginatively construct such an experience out of related ones, so that the words will be genuinely meaningful to us. Even knowing Merriam-

Webster's definition of "tiger moth" as "A moth of a family (Arctiidae) typically stout-bodied with broad striped or spotted wings" will not help us to any distinct image unless we have also seen a tiger moth or something like it. Hence imagery usually recalls, rather than originates, mental impressions, so that the reader is implicated in the creation of the poetic image. The reader will be responsive to the extent that his experience has provided him with a rich stock of images. This creative participation of the reader in the poetic process should not lead us to suppose that the able reader weaves his own fancies out of the poem, but only that he responds fully to the stimuli actually in the poem.

The foregoing illustrations have dealt with *visual imagery*, the most frequent kind. Yet poetry also appeals to other senses. These lines from another stanza of "The Eve of St. Agnes" contain images appealing to what we loosely call the sense of feeling:

> Soon, trembling in her soft and chilly nest,
> In sort of wakeful swoon, perplexed she lay,
> Until the poppied warmth of sleep oppressed
> Her soothéd limbs, and soul fatigued away; . . .

"Trembling," "soft," "chilly," "wakeful swoon," "poppied" (i.e., like the drowsiness produced by opium), "warmth," "soothéd" all suggest the sensations preceding sleep. Since it is dark, none of the images is visual. In Robert Frost's "Birches" these remarkable tactile images occur:

> . . . life is too much like a pathless wood
> Where your face burns and tickles with the cobwebs
> Broken across it, and one eye is weeping
> From a twig's having lashed across it open.

Auditory imagery is also fairly frequent. It may be produced by the naming and describing of sounds as in this example, again from "The Eve of St. Agnes":

> The boisterous, midnight, festive clarion,
> The kettle-drum, and far-heard clarinet,
> Affray his ears, though but in dying tone:—
> The hall door shuts again, and all the noise is gone.

Elsewhere Keats reinforces auditory imagery by imitating natural sounds in the sounds of his words:

> The silver, snarling trumpets 'gan to chide: . . .
>
> .   .   .   .
>
> . . . meantime the frost-wind blows
> Like Love's alarum *pattering the sharp sleet*
> Against the window-panes; . . .

This device, which we shall discuss more fully in a later section, is known as *onomatopoeia*.

The other senses—taste and smell—in the traditional list of five are less frequently involved in imagery, and they almost invariably operate by reminding us of our own sense experiences or by comparing a novel taste or odor to a familiar one. In "Thyrsis" Matthew Arnold writes, "Soon   shall   we   have . . . /Sweet-William   with   his homely cottage smell,/And stocks in fragrant blow" and later, "And scent of hay new mown." The vocabulary describing flavors and odors is very small compared with that for shapes or colors.

Imagery, then, can be produced by names, descriptions, rhythms ("the tolling tolling bells' perpetual clang"), intellectual associations ("The music, yearning like a God in pain"), or several of these devices working together. Finally, imagery is one of the chief means by which literature achieves the concrete, specific, and hence moving and impressive quality we have attributed to it.

C. Figurative Language

Another important quality of poetic diction is *figurative language. Figures of speech*, however varied, have one thing in common: they deal with something by relating it to something else. The relationship and the effects produced by establishing them are numerous. We isolate here only the most frequent figures; yet these classes will account for most of the figures we shall identify. More important than classifying figures is determining the effects they produce.

1. *Metaphor*

When a writer or speaker asserts that something is, or is equivalent to, something in most ways actually unlike it, the figure is called a *metaphor*. Consider the following brief poem by Sir Walter Ralegh:

What Is Our Life?

What is our life? a play of passion;
Our mirth, the music of division;
Our mothers' wombs the tiring-houses be
Where we are dressed for this short comedy.
Heaven the judicious sharp spectator is,
That sits and marks still who doth act amiss;
Our graves that hide us from the searching sun
Are like drawn curtains when the play is done.
Thus march we playing to our latest rest;
Only we die in earnest—that's no jest.   10

Ralegh's assertion, in the first line, that our life is "a play of passion" is a metaphor because it equates "life" and "play." Frequently the *principal term*—here "life"—is abstract, vague, intangible, or unfamiliar, whereas the *secondary term*—"play" in our example—is concrete, definite, and familiar. The effect, then, is to make the intangible principal term vivid and available for discussion. Since the two terms are basically unlike, the metaphor throws great emphasis on the qualities they do share, as when Ralegh calls attention to the brevity and triviality of stage plays and then imputes these characteristics to life, "this short comedy." Note that Ralegh has produced an *extended metaphor* by asserting, with some ingenuity, that the identity he has perceived between life and a play also holds between subsidiary parts of each spectacle: laughter

is musical accompaniment; wombs are dressing rooms
(both are places of preparation); Heaven is the spectator
who judges; graves are the curtains which fall at the end
of the spectacle. Finally, the metaphor also frequently
passes judgment on the principal term by comparing it to
a secondary term chosen with a particular attitude in
mind. Ralegh's "play of passion" becomes a "short comedy," to suggest, somewhat sadly perhaps, that life is not
as serious as we might like to think it.

Even though Ralegh refers casually to life as "this short
comedy" without using the full form of the metaphor,
"life is a short comedy," none of the metaphoric force is
lost. Such a figure is called an *implicit metaphor*. In
Tennyson's "Ulysses" the hero says, "I will drink/Life to
the lees." Here the implicit metaphor that pictures a man
thirsty for experience drinking down his life is reinforced
by "lees," the sediment in the bottom of the cup.

Much of our language is metaphoric in origin, though
we are inclined to forget the original comparisons that
gave rise—sometimes centuries ago—to new words. As
Emerson says in "Nature," "Every word which is used to
express a moral or intellectual fact, if traced to its root, is
found to be borrowed from some material appearance.
'Right' means 'straight'; 'wrong' means 'twisted.' 'Spirit'
primarily means 'wind'; 'transgression,' the 'crossing of a
line'; 'supercilious,' the 'raising of the eyebrow.' " Slang
often begins as witty implicit metaphor but soon becomes
so worn through overuse that we forget its metaphoric
origin. The result, like such standard phrases as "the arm
of a chair" or "the brow of a cliff," is a *dead metaphor*.
The person who first said, "Don't monkey with that" had
a brilliant satiric insight, but few of us now imagine a
meddlesome little animal when we use the tired phrase.
Similarly, many apparently abstract terms are dead implicit metaphors. With a little effort we are able to remember that the phrase, "grasp an idea" (or slang "catch on")
suggests that the mental operation is much like taking
hold of a solid object with the hand. We may, however,

be unaware that "comprehension" embodies the same metaphor until we remember what "prehension" is and that elephants have "prehensile" trunks.

In reading poetry we should be alert to the metaphoric implications of words so that we can fully understand and enjoy its concrete vividness. We usually understand the word "expatiate" to mean "to enlarge upon a theme in speech or writing." This meaning embodies a dead metaphor based upon an earlier concrete sense of the word, to range freely over an area, which was once used in hunting to denote beating a field for game. (The etymology of the word suggests this meaning: *ex*, out + *spatiari*, to walk about, from *spatium*, space.) At the opening of "An Essay on Man," Pope reanimates this dead metaphor:

> Let us . . .
> Expatiate free o'er all this scene of Man;
> A mighty maze! but not without a plan;
> A Wild, where weeds and flow'rs promiscuous shoot;
> Or Garden, tempting with forbidden fruit.
> Together let us beat this ample field,
> Try what the open, what the covert yield;
> The latent tracts, the giddy heights, explore
> Of all who blindly creep, or sightless soar;
> Eye Nature's walks, shoot Folly as it flies,   10
> And catch the Manners living as they rise; . . .

Throughout this passage Pope is inviting a friend to join him in discussing man's condition; that is, to expatiate, or expand, upon an abstract theme. In representing this enterprise as a hunt, Pope is taking advantage of the metaphoric relationship of the older concrete and the newer abstract meanings of the word. The metaphor is extended by fitting subordinate parts of the abstract undertaking into the concrete representation of it: human life becomes a varied landscape, wild but not planless; men become creeping or soaring creatures; follies and manners become game birds to be shot down as they are flushed from cover.

Some writers, incidentally, use *metaphor* as a generic

term synonymous with *figurative language* to include the following figures as varieties.

A figure of speech closely related to metaphor is *simile*, in which similarity, rather than identity, is asserted. The figure includes one of several words such as "like," "as," or "than." Thus "Our graves . . . are *like* drawn curtains" is a simile. In the following example the poet is interested in a single quality—swiftness—which identifies the two terms of his simile, and a point-by-point comparison like that in "What Is Our Life?" would be fruitless:

> Swift as the weaver's shuttle fleet our years.

A formal variety of the simile is the *epic simile*, so named from its frequent occurrence in the Homeric epics. It is developed at some length according to a fairly strict formula: *as* a person in mythology, history, or the Bible once did something (or as a thing in nature does), *so* now a character in the epic does something similar. Milton uses the device in *Paradise Lost*, the great Christian epic:

> As when a flock
> Of ravenous fowl, though many a league remote,
> Against the day of battle, to a field
> Where armies lie encamped, come flying, lured
> With scent of living carcasses designed
> For death, the following day, in bloody fight:
> So scented the grim Feature,* and upturned
> His nostril wide into the murky air,
> Sagacious of his quarry from so far.

The secondary term following "as" or "as when" alludes to material presumably familiar to Milton's readers and hence already available to explain or describe the new matter of the principal term following "so." Sometimes only the secondary term is expanded.

An elaborately ingenious metaphor or simile in which

---

* Death.

the things compared are more than usually unlike each
other is called a *conceit.* "What Is Our Life?" may be
considered a conceit because of its ingenuity. The work of
the seventeenth-century metaphysical school is charac-
terized by the *metaphysical conceit,* an often strained asso-
ciation of almost wholly dissimilar things. Here is a famous
example in which John Donne compares the souls of two
lovers to the legs of a draftsman's compass:

> Our two souls therefore, which are one,
>   Though I must go, endure not yet
> A breach, but an expansion,
>   Like gold to airy thinness beat.
>
> If they be two, they are two so
>   As stiff twin compasses are two,
> Thy soul, the fixt foot, makes no show
>   To move, but doth, if th' other do.
>
> And though it in the center sit,
>   Yet when the other far doth roam,
> It leans, and hearkens after it,
>   And grows erect, as that comes home.
>
> Such wilt thou be to me, who must
>   Like th' other foot, obliquely run;
> Thy firmness makes my circle just,
>   And makes me end, where I begun.

Metaphor and simile may be combined in a chain or a
nest of comparisons one within the other. Arnold's "Dover
Beach" shows some interesting uses of linked metaphors
and similes.

Dover Beach

> The sea is calm to-night,
> The tide is full, the moon lies fair
> Upon the Straits;—on the French coast, the light
> Gleams, and is gone; the cliffs of England stand,
> Glimmering and vast, out in the tranquil bay.

Come to the window, sweet is the night air!
Only, from the long line of spray
Where the ebb meets the moon-blanched sand,
Listen! you hear the grating roar
Of pebbles which the waves suck back, and fling,   10
At their return, up the high strand,
Begin, and cease, and then again begin,
With tremulous cadence slow, and bring
The eternal note of sadness in.

Sophocles long ago
Heard it on the Ægean, and it brought
Into his mind the turbid ebb and flow
Of human misery; we
Find also in the sound a thought,
Hearing it by this distant northern sea.   20

The sea of faith
Was once, too, at the full, and round earth's shore
Lay like the folds of a bright girdle furled;
But now I only hear
Its melancholy, long, withdrawing roar,
Retreating to the breath
Of the night-wind down the vast edges drear
And naked shingles of the world.

Ah, love, let us be true
To one another! for the world, which seems   30
To lie before us like a land of dreams,
So various, so beautiful, so new,
Hath really neither joy, nor love, nor light,
Nor certitude, nor peace, nor help for pain;
And we are here as on a darkling plain
Swept with confused alarms of struggle and flight,
Where ignorant armies clash by night.

The first thirteen lines are notable for effective imagery, but they have virtually no metaphoric overtones. The fourteenth line speaks of "The eternal note of sadness," a phrase that obliquely identifies the sound of the waves with the expression of human emotion. The next four lines explicitly attribute to Sophocles a metaphoric identification of the motion of the sea and the tides of human suffering. Lines 21 and 22 offer a different metaphor: faith is a sea that ebbs and flows. In the next line a simile likens this sea of faith to "the folds of a bright girdle furled," so that the principal term of the simile is itself a metaphor. Lines 24 through 28 drop the simile of the girdle and return to the metaphor of faith as a sea ebbing down the graveled beaches of the world. Lines 30 through 34 contain what might be considered a negative simile: the speaker denies that the world is like the land of dreams it appears to be. As an alternative he proposes the simile of the world as a nighttime battlefield where men fight without knowing their enemies or their aims.

2. *Metonymy and Synecdoche*

Two other important figures related to metaphor are *metonymy* and *synecdoche*, both occasionally very striking, but far less frequent in occurrence than metaphor or simile. Metonymy is the use of an attribute of an object or of something closely associated with it to represent that object. The following stanza by James Shirley illustrates this figure:

> The glories of our blood and state
>   Are shadows, not substantial things;
> There is no armour against Fate;
>   Death lays his icy hand on kings:
>   Sceptre and crown
>   Must tumble down,
>   And in the dust be equal made
> With the poor crooked scythe and spade.

Here "sceptre and crown" stand for rulers, while "scythe and spade" stand for commoners. The choice of these emblems and implements has a twofold effect: First, the concrete terms are more vivid—that is, they produce more clearly realized images—than the more general terms we have substituted for them. Second, the contrasting of these implements emphasizes the disparity of social status between royalty and commoners. The objects are in the one case actual, and in the other appropriate, though not actual, badges of rank.

Synecdoche is so nearly like metonymy that most of our comments on that figure apply here as well. Synecdoche substitutes a significant part of something for the thing itself, as when Shirley uses "blood" to stand for lineage or race. Similarly, "farm hands" or "loud mouths" are whole people, all right, but the speaker chooses the parts that interest him in a given connection.

3. Personification

Another figure somewhat similar to metaphor is *personification*. Here abstraction is endowed with the qualities of a human being in such a way as to render a normally disembodied idea dramatically effective. Shirley's "Death lays his icy hand on kings" uses one of the most common personifications but rescues it from banality by precise and appropriate imagery. Less obvious is the personification in the preceding line—"There is no armour against Fate"—but the capital letter calls attention to the device. Personification lies at the heart of *allegory*, which we shall encounter in another connection.

Personification is often involved in *apostrophe*, a rhetorical device in which the poet speaks to a personified abstraction or to an absent person:

> Eternal Spirit of the chainless mind!
> Brightest in Dungeons, Liberty! thou art,
> For there thy habitation is the heart— . . .
>
> .   .   .   .
>
> Milton, thou shouldst be living at this hour;
> England hath need of thee; . . .

D. Rhetorical Devices

Next we consider a group of *rhetorical devices*, intellectual stratagems rather than figure- or image-making maneuvers. They convey attitudes and sometimes imply underlying assumptions of a kind not associated with the figures we have dealt with in the preceding section.

1. *Hyperbole and Understatement*

Hyperbole is deliberate, and often outrageous, exaggeration. It may be used to magnify a fact or an emotion in such a way as to attribute great importance to it:

> Hark, how my Celia, with the choice
> Music of her hand and voice
> Stills the loud wind; and makes the wild
> Incenséd boar and panther mild;
> Mark how these statues like men move,
> Whilst men with wonder, statues prove!
> This stiff rock bends to worship her,
> That idol turns idolater.

In other uses, hyperbole may be ironic and have the final effect of deflating the significance of the matter treated:

> Then flashed the living lightning from her eyes,
> And screams of horror rend th'affrighted skies.
> Not louder shrieks to pitying heaven are cast,
> When husbands, or when lapdogs breathe their last; . . .

The juxtaposing of husbands and lapdogs imparts a comic tone to the whole passage and makes clear that we are not to take the "living lightning" very seriously.

The opposite device is known as *understatement*. Here the effect is almost always to magnify the matter discussed, by implying that the means of expression is inadequate to the task:

> We know, too, they are very fond of war,
>   A pleasure—like all pleasures—rather dear; . . .

Calling war "rather dear" is understatement; calling it a pleasure—which it certainly is not—is *irony*. Understatement is usually ironic, as this simultaneous occurrence of the devices suggests.

In a very general way, irony is the quality that arises from a discrepancy between just expectations and actualities. Thus we may speak of circumstances as ironic if we feel that we have a right to expect some kind of success and are denied that success in a perversely appropriate way. Such irony may be depicted in a literary work, but literature may also show an ironic view by employing *verbal irony*. This rhetorical device is the use of language that on the surface appears to mean something innocent but that has for the person sufficiently informed—either the speaker or the hearer, or perhaps both—a somewhat or even quite different import. Shelley's "Ozymandias" illustrates both kinds of irony. The contrast between the pride of the ambitious "king of kings" and the "decay of that colossal wreck" amid its "lone and level sands" is an example of the *irony of circumstance*. The inscription on the base of the monument illustrates verbal irony. "Look on my works ye mighty, and despair!" meant to Ozymandias, "Despair of matching my achievements," but to the reader, who sees the sad end to which all human vanity must come, the message means, "Despair of defying time's destruction."

Another device resulting in ironic understatement is *anticlimax*. Normally the most important or climactic element of an utterance comes at the end—of a sentence, stanza, or poem. When an important item is followed by a trivial one, we experience an intellectual and emotional deflation. If such anticlimax is deliberate and controlled, it produces comic or satiric effects. Pope uses this device brilliantly in his mock epic, "The Rape of the Lock":

> Or stain her honor or her new brocade; . . .

Taking advantage of the metaphorically double sense of stain, Pope links a loss of virtue with spoiling a frock as though the two were of equal importance. Since we know that they are not, we recognize the moral shallowness of a society that fails to distinguish degrees of transgression.

The statement of something as the negative of its contrary is called *litotes*; it usually has the effect of understatement. In E. A. Robinson's "How Annandale Went Out," the narrator says, "And the sight was not so fair/As one or two that I had seen elsewhere" to tell us that the sight of his dying friend was one of the most horrible he had ever seen.

2. Ambiguity

A number of devices involve *ambiguity*, or what we commonly call double meaning. In scientific prose, ambiguity is considered a fault, but in literature ambiguity may produce humor, or enrich meaning, or reflect the writer's perception of the complexity of life. In "How Annandale Went Out" the narrator says, "Now view yourself as I was, on the spot." By "on the spot" he means that he was at the scene, but he implies also the slang sense of the phrase—that he was forced to make a decision. The ambiguity of the phrase reflects the opposition between the demands of his professional code and the appeal to his human sympathies. The *pun* is a familiar kind of ambiguity—that is, use of words with more than one possible meaning—for a comic effect. Puns are of many sorts, ranging from those exploiting vague similarities in sound, through plays on distinctly separate meanings of what appears to be the same word in various settings, to the use of such etymological and metaphorical relationships as we discovered in "expatiate" and "stain." Ben Jonson, in "To the Memory of . . . Shakespeare" puns on the name of his subject:

> . . . his well-turnéd and true-filéd lines;
> In each of which he seems to *shake a lance*,
> As brandished at the eyes of ignorance.

(Remember that a brand is a sword, and that to brandish is to wave as a sword.) Shakespeare puns on his own first name in line 13 of his "Sonnet CXLIII" (which, by the way, takes the form of an epic simile):

CXLIII

Lo! as a careful housewife runs to catch
One of her feathered creatures broke away,
Sets down her babe and makes all swift dispatch
In pursuit of the thing she would have stay,
Whilst her neglected child holds her in chase,
Cries to catch her whose busy care is bent
To follow that which flies before her face,
Not prizing her poor infant's discontent;
So runn'st thou after that which flies from thee,
Whilst I, thy babe, chase thee afar behind;   10
But if thou catch thy hope, turn back to me,
And play the mother's part, kiss me, be kind:
So will I pray that thou mayst have thy *Will*,
If thou turn back, and my loud crying still.

These examples are little more than good fun, but a pun can also contribute to the idea of a poem. In a poem written during the depression, a modern version of a Renaissance poem, Day Lewis puns on two senses (not etymologically or metaphorically related) of the word "tire." An archaic sense of the word is "attire," to clothe (recall "tiring-houses" in "What Is Our Life?"):

> . . . not silken dress
> But toil shall *tire* thy loveliness.

In this instance the pun contributes to the poem's bitter comedy. In the next example the pun is part of a metaphor, and the two senses of the word arose originally by a metaphoric transfer of meaning from physical objects to an intangible mental condition. George Herbert's "The Windows" pictures man as a window in God's temple:

> Lord, how can man preach thy eternal word?
> He is a brittle *crazy* glass, . . .

As applied to glass, "crazy" (our modern form is "crazed") means covered with a network of tiny cracks. Within the metaphor the word applies to both glass and man; as applied to man it means insane or at least deficient in divine wisdom. The same pun appears in the slang term "cracked." In each of these examples a shift in our understanding of the key word changes the sense of the whole sentence.

A *paradox* is a statement which is either apparently self-contradictory or at odds with ordinary experience, and yet reveals a truth normally hidden:

> Stone walls do not a prison make,
>   Nor iron bars a cage; . . .

Usually some unexpressed condition explains the paradox. In this quotation the reader understands, even though he does not articulate the point, that the spirit is free even though the body is confined. A special kind of paradox is *oxymoron*, the associating of opposite terms in a single expression, usually to reflect a mixture of attitudes toward an event. Thus Shakespeare's "Parting is such sweet sorrow" conveys Juliet's mixed feelings in the phrase, "sweet sorrow."

3. *Ellipsis*

Ellipsis is the omission of words necessary for grammatical completeness but readily supplied by the reader's imagination. In poetry ellipsis is one means of gaining compression by avoiding wordy constructions. Our earlier passage from "An Essay on Man" included the phrase "giddy heights." The hilltops do not suffer from dizziness but produce it in human beings. Yet no confusion results from Pope's shorthand version of what would otherwise be an awkward locution. Ellipsis also has a tendency to transfer the characteristics of one object to another so that it may take on some of the qualities of metaphor. In reading the stanza from "The Eve of St. Agnes" offered for its examples of imagery, we may have passed over the phrase "twilight saints." In the context of the stanza it is clear that the saints are pictured in a stained-glass window and are "twilight" saints because the interior of the chapel is dim in the filtered light. The phrase may also suggest, though, that holy things are shadowed by the murders of queens and kings.

III

The Form of Poetry

One of the qualities which chiefly distinguishes literature from nonliterary writing is the close relationship—
indeed, the actual fusion—of form and idea. We shall
sometimes pretend that we can detach the meaning from
the form of a work, but we had better remember that this
maneuver is preliminary to apprehending the whole piece
and that the extracted "meaning"—by which term we
probably designate a prose paraphrase—is far less than the
total work of literature. Drama and fiction both have
significant form, for the arrangement of events, the prose
style—its diction, figures, and rhythms—and the selection
of detail are all part of the meaning of the work. But in
poetry the union of form and content is so intimate that,
although the extraction of a theme is unsatisfactory for the
other genres, it is almost impossible in a successful poem.
A poem is not an idea carried in a basket woven of sentences; it is an organism whose substance does not exist
separate from the shape that it has.

A. Sound Values

Among the most striking elements of poetic form are its
sound values. No one of these elements is indispensable to

poetry, but each of them is used often enough to warrant its treatment here.

1. *Rhyme*

Lines of verse are said to *rhyme*—or to *have rhyme*, or to have a *rhyme scheme*—when the ends of their final words have identical sounds. By the "end" of a word we mean here the vowel of the last accented syllable and any sounds that may follow it:

> Come with bows bent and with emptying of quivers,
> > Maiden most perfect, lady of light,
> With a noise of winds and many rivers,
> > With a clamour of waters, and with might;
> Bind on thy sandals, O thou most fleet,
> Over the splendour and speed of thy feet;
> For the faint east quickens, the wan west shivers,
> > Round the feet of the day and the feet of the night.

Here "quivers," "rivers," "shivers"; "light," "might," "night"; and "fleet," "feet" are rhyming groups. In each of these clusters both pronunciation and spelling coincide. Since rhyming is a matter of sound, though, a difference in spelling is of no consequence so long as the various spellings represent the same sound:

> There be none of Beauty's daughters
> > With a magic like thee;
> And like music on the waters
> > Is thy sweet voice to me:
>
> .   .   .   .
>
> With a full but soft emotion
> Like the swell of Summer's ocean.

A number of effects are possible by the use of rhyme. One of these is simply the pleasure that we experience in the chiming of like sounds. In addition, a pattern of rhymes established early in a poem arouses expectation as each successive rhyming word of a new set occurs so that the arrival of the second rhyming word of the pair fulfills that expectation. One kind of aesthetic enjoyment lies in gratifying the expectation of pattern.

We have described so far the usual—what might be regarded as the normal—condition of rhyme; there are, though, a number of interesting variations. When the accented vowel is in the final syllable of the line—and again, this is the usual practice—the rhymes are said to be *masculine*. The effect is sometimes thought to be stronger, the utterance more positive, than in the other situation. When one or two unaccented syllables follow the accented syllable in the rhyming words, the rhyme is *feminine*. The movement of the lines is then graceful and continuous, without the firm close produced by a masculine rhyme. The more frequent kind of feminine rhyme, that of two syllables, is called *double rhyme. Triple rhyme* is the variety of feminine rhyme in which two unaccented syllables follow the accented syllable and all three rhyme with a similar arrangement in a nearby line. More often than not triple rhyme is used for humorous verse; we delight in the poet's display of his ingenuity, an ingenuity that often serves a flippant or satiric attitude. The effect is especially ludicrous if the challenge of a trisyllabic word can be met only by putting together two or three words to produce a synthetic rhyming word or if the rhyming contract can be filled only by warping the pronunciation or stress of a phrase. The following stanza from Byron's *Don Juan* shows masculine rhyme in lines 1, 3, and 5; double feminine rhyme in lines 2, 4, and 6; and triple feminine rhyme in lines 7 and 8:

> 'Tis pity learned virgins ever wed
>   With persons of no sort of education,
> Or gentlemen, who, though well born and bred,
>   Grow tired of scientific conversation;
> I don't choose to say much upon this head,
>   I'm a plain man, and in a single station,
> But—Oh! ye lords of ladies intellectual,
> Inform us truly, have they not hen-pecked you all?

A special variety of rhyme is the *inexact* or *slant rhyme*. Here the sounds of the rhyming words are not identical but only similar, and they may be more similar or less in one instance or another. In one poem, for example, Emily Dickinson slant rhymes "pain"-"tune," "know"-"do," "obey"-"bee," and "come"-"fame." Inexact rhymes retain the general suggestion of pattern produced by the regular recurrence of like sounds, but they do not insist on it. The pattern operates unobtrusively without calling attention to itself. Slant rhyme is especially useful to link very brief lines, for it binds them together without producing the jingling effect that results when the precise and predictable rhyming word comes around too soon. In addition, inexact rhymes have something of the effect of slight dissonances in music; they support moods of tartness, uncertainty, or melancholy rather than of sweetness, assurance, or joy. Emily Dickinson used them liberally, and twentieth-century poets have found them congenial to certain modern attitudes.

We usually expect to find rhymes in the final position of lines of verse. This customary use is called *end rhyme*. Some poets enrich their verbal melody by placing a word within the line (usually at or near the middle) to rhyme with the final word. Such *internal rhyme* enhances the binding effect of rhymes; it may also give great stress to certain lines if most lines in the poem do not share this quality.

> The fair breeze blew, the white foam flew,
> The furrow followed free;
> We were the first that ever burst
> Into that silent sea.
>
> Down dropped the breeze, the sails dropped down,
> 'Twas sad as sad could be;
> And we did speak only to break
> The silence of the sea!

In the first of these stanzas the first and third lines contain exact internal rhymes: "blew"-"flew"; "first"-"burst." In

the second stanza the reader expects the final word of the
first line to rhyme with "breeze," but he is disappointed.
In the third line "speak"-"break" looks like a rhyme (this
peculiarity is sometimes called an *eye rhyme*), but it too
is a disappointment. Note that these manipulations of
the rhymes are related to the subject matter of the stanzas.

We should note at this point that the usual practice in
marking *rhyme schemes* is to label the first rhyming line
and each successive line that rhymes with it with a small *a*.
The next line that ends with a different rhyme is marked
b, as are all successive lines that rhyme with it. This system
may be extended indefinitely, although letters beyond *g*
are rarely needed. All lines without rhyming companions
are labeled *x*.

2. Alliteration and Assonance

A sound effect closely related to rhyme is *alliteration*, or
the repetition of a sound in the initial position of various
words, or of a consonant sound within the words.

In the first of the stanzas just quoted from "The Rime
of the Ancient Mariner," note the intertwining of several
alliterative sequences involving *f*, *b*, *w*, and *s*:

> The *f*air *b*reeze *b*lew, the white *f*oam *f*lew,
> The *f*urrow *f*ollowed *f*ree;
> *W*e *w*ere the *f*irst that ever *b*urst
> Into that *s*ilent *s*ea.

This heavy use of alliteration coincides with the use of
internal rhyme to impart great intensity to the lines. In
the second of the stanzas the alliterative sequences of *d*
and *s* are somewhat less intense in keeping with the emotional slackening of the lines. In addition, a relationship
may be asserted between words beginning with the same
sound, as in "sad," "silence," and "sea." Similarly A. E.
Housman uses alliteration to link beer and a bard, thus
belittling the importance of the poet:

> Oh, many a peer of England brews
> Livelier liquor than the Muse,

> And *malt* does more than *Milton* can
> To justify God's ways to man.

Finally, certain emotions may be echoed by the repetition of appropriate consonants:

> Like to the Pontic sea,
> Whose icy current and compulsive course
> Ne'er feels retiring ebb, but keeps due on
> To the Propontic and the Hellespont;
> Even so my bloody thoughts, with violent pace,
> Shall ne'er look back, ne'er ebb to humble love,
> Till that a capable and wide revenge
> Swallow them up.

This is Othello, maddened by Iago's insinuations, swearing revenge upon his wife's supposed seducer. His violence expresses itself in a spluttering outburst of explosive consonant sounds (*b, d, k, p, t*), intermixed with hissing *s* sounds.

We usually think of alliteration as involving repetition of the same sounds, but consonants merely similar, rather than identical, may also be alliterative. Thus *n* and *m* sounds may be interlinked to strengthen the alliterative effect:

> The night shakes them round me in legions.

When the writer varies the surrounding consonant sounds, but repeats vowel sounds, the device is known as *assonance*. Although assonance is used as frequently as alliteration, its effects are more subtle. Thus the reader is less likely to be immediately aware of this additional means of distributing emphasis or imparting emotional tone:

> Cold eyelids that hide like a jewel
> Hard eyes that grow soft for an hour; . . .

In identifying patterns of alliteration and assonance, we are concerned with similarity of sounds, however spelled (*eye*, hide), not with identical spellings that produce different sounds (hot, loft).

3. Onomatopoeia

Onomatopoeia is the imitation of natural sounds in the sounds of words. Many common words, such as "hum" or "clatter" or "moo," sound somewhat like the sounds they name. In poetry such words are only one means to suggest natural sounds. Rhythm ("Half a league, half a league, half a league onward" to represent hoofbeats, for example), the sounds of words even though they do not refer to natural sounds, and both alliteration and assonance may contribute an onomatopoetic effect. In the following passage from Tennyson's "Morte d'Arthur" all of these elements combine to imitate the sound of a knight in armor striding over rocky ground:

> Dry clashed his harness in the icy caves
> And barren chasms, and all to left and right
> The bare black cliff clanged round him, as he based
> His feet on juts of slippery crag that rang
> Sharp-smitten with the dint of armed heels— . . .

It should be noted, of course, that this effect, like the others we have discussed, will operate only if the sense of the passage reinforces and is reinforced by the sound devices.

B. Versification

All of these "sound effects" are related to the structural practices known collectively as *versification*, including rhythm, meter, and stanza form.

1. Rhythm and Meter

An important element in all language is *rhythm*. We may define it as the regular recurrence of *accent* or *stress*. In any polysyllabic word in English, one of the syllables receives a greater stress than the others. Pronounce these words in sequence: "photograph," "photographer," "photographic." Which syllable is most heavily stressed in each word? Precisely what have you done to lend stress to a particular syllable? Note that stress consists of greater than normal volume of sound, an elevation in vowel pitch, and a slight increase in the time during which the vowel of the stressed syllable is intoned. In addition to the *primary stress* in a polysyllabic word, one or more of the other syllables may receive a *secondary stress*. Marking a primary stress with a single accent mark and a secondary stress with a double mark, we would indicate the accenting of the words cited earlier as follows: phó·to·gráph; pho·tóg·ra·phér; phó·to·gráph·ic. In the early stages of our study, we may consider all stressed syllables as equal; later we shall want to distinguish not only primary and secondary, but also several degrees of stress.

Monosyllabic words may be thought of as stressed when they stand alone, but, when associated with other words in phrases, they are stressed or unstressed according to the meaning of the phrase: "dówn the stréet." In turn, when phrases are grouped into sentences, the stresses in the phrases may shift: "As we wálked down the stréet, we mét twó of our friénds." Again, the stressing of a sentence may be changed, without any change in its wording, to suggest different meanings by different intonation patterns: "[On the way up the street, we saw no one;] as we wálked dówn the stréet, we mét twó of our friénds." The alternation of stressed and unstressed syllables, then, is the rhythm of all language, including prose as well as poetry. In prose the distribution of stresses may be very irregular—that is, few or no or many unstressed syllables may fall between the stressed syllables, and there may be no discernible pattern to the recurrence of stresses.

In verse we can usually identify an ideal regular pattern

of stressed and unstressed syllables. The opening lines of
Coleridge's "Frost at Midnight" show a pattern of stresses
with few complications:

> The Frost performs its secret ministry,
>
> Unhelped by any wind. The owlet's cry
>
> Came loud—and hark, again! loud as before.
>
> The inmates of my cottage, all at rest,
>
> Have left me to that solitude, which suits
>
> Abstruser musings: save that at my side
>
> My cradled infant slumbers peacefully.
>
> 'Tis calm indeed! so calm, that it disturbs
>
> And vexes meditation with its strange
>
> And extreme silentness.   10

In six of the ten lines the pattern is the same: unstressed
and stressed syllables precisely alternate. In three of the
remaining lines this pattern is disturbed at only one point,
so that even in these lines the usual alternation is dominant. The ideal pattern is called the *meter* of the verse,
and we call it ideal, for the actual distribution of stresses
rarely conforms to the pattern very long without a mo-
mentary deviation. Still, there is a general tendency which
may be thought of as the meter—the ideal pattern—struggling to confine the logical rhythms of the sentences. We
can usually identify the ideal pattern without great difficulty and discover the effect of the degree of conformity
of the *actual rhythm* to the ideal meter.

It is customary to divide the metric line into units called
feet, each *foot* usually containing one stressed syllable and
its associated unstressed syllables. (In the *spondee* both
syllables are stressed.) The most important foot in English verse is the *iamb*, or *iambic* foot, consisting of an unstressed syllable followed by a stressed one ($\smile\,\prime$):

> Mў heárt | ĭs líke | ă síng | ĭng bírd
> Whŏse nést | ĭs ín | ă wá | tĕred shóot.

By far the greater bulk of English verse is written in a basically iambic meter. Several other meters, of the number of possible ones, are of sufficient frequency to be identified here. The *trochee* or *trochaic foot* is another two-syllable foot; the accented syllable comes first (´˘):

> Thére thĕy | aŕe, mў | fíftў | mén ănd | wómĕn
> Námĭng | mé thĕ | fíftў | póemŝ | fínĭshĕd!

Two trisyllabic feet appear with some frequency in English verse. The commoner of these is the *anapest* (˘˘´), which, like the iamb, is called a *rising meter* because the accent occurs at the end of the foot:

> Fŏr thĕ móon | nĕvĕr beáms | wĭthŏut bríng | ĭng mĕ dreáms
> Ŏf thĕ beáu | tĭfŭl Án | năbĕl Leé;
> Ănd thĕ staŕs | nĕvĕr ríse | bŭt Ĭ feél | thĕ bríght eýes
> Ŏf thĕ beáu | tĭfŭl Án | năbĕl Leé.

The effect of anapestic lines is often light and swift. The lines also tend to fall into singsong, especially when the verse is thoroughly regular as it is here, or when the regularity is reinforced by internal rhymes, such as "beams," "dreams" in the first of these lines and "rise," "eyes" in the third. In this example the effect is further strengthened by the identity of the second and fourth lines so that the poem can be read acceptably, if at all, only by varying the intensity of stresses and muting the ideal meter through a greater than usual attention to the logical rhythm.

The trisyllabic foot in *falling meter* is called a *dactyl* (´˘˘). It is the least frequently used of the four major English meters and is more important as a source of substitute feet than as a predominant meter. Note also that

since the foot ends in two unaccented syllables, the rhyme
must be either feminine triple rhyme, or the unusual and
awkward rhyming of unaccented syllables only. Hence,
dactylic lines are likely to be unrhymed, as in *Evangeline*,
or a substitution is made for the final dactyl. Thomas
Hood's "The Bridge of Sighs" shows the triple feminine
rhyme in lines 1 and 3 of each stanza and the substitution
of a single accent in lines 2 and 4:

> One more un | fortunate
> Weary of | breath,
> Rashly im | portunate,
> Gone to her | death!

Several kinds of variation on these basic meters are possible. Two later lines of Christina Rosetti's "A Birthday,"
which we have cited as an example of iambic meter, show
a frequent kind of variation:

> Raise me | a dais | of silk | and down;
> Hang it | with vair | and pur | ple dyes; . . .

Here the imperative requires stress on the verb, which is
the first syllable of each line, so that the first foot is a
trochee. Note also that some diversity of reading is possible
here: "dais" may be pronounced as one syllable with a
long *a*, in which case the foot is a normal iamb. If, however, the reader chooses to pronounce the word with two
syllables ("da·is"), as is usual, the third foot might be
thought of as having two unstressed syllables before the
stressed one ("-is of silk"), in which case it would be an
anapest. Actually the tendency would be to slur "-is" and
"of" together into a single unstressed syllable so that once
again we would have an iambic foot.

Other variations appear in the following basically trochaic stanza:

> Out ŭ | pón it! | Í hăve | lóved ˘
> Thrée whóle | dayś tŏ | gétheř;
> And ăm | líke tŏ | lóve thrée | móre, ˘
> Íf iť | próve fáir | wéatheř.

Notice that a trochaic foot at the end of a line produces a feminine rhyme, as in the second and fourth lines. If the poet wishes to avoid excessive use of feminine rhymes, he may leave the lines unrhymed as Browning does in the sample of trochaic meter we cited earlier. More often he produces a masculine rhyme by omitting the final unstressed syllable as in lines 1 and 3 of the present example. Thus he gains the advantage of beginning the line with a stress, as he could not with an ordinary iambic line (though he often gets this benefit by substituting a trochee for the first iamb), and at the same time ends the line with a stress to secure a masculine rhyme. Obviously there will occasionally be a difference of opinion as to whether the basic meter is iambic or trochaic, the one or the other modified by any of a number of substitutions or variations.

In addition, several feet in this stanza contain two stressed syllables. This foot is called a *spondee*, or *spondaic foot* (´´). It is used as a substitute foot where great emphasis is to be placed on a phrase, or where an abrupt, forceful movement is appropriate. Only rarely does it provide the prevailing meter of a line.

Sometimes the shifting of an accent will leave a foot of two unaccented syllables:

> And ŏf | ten fŏr | púre doúbt | and dréad
> Shĕ sóbbed, | madĕ gíd | dў ĭn | thĕ héad.

Such a foot is called a *pyrrhus* or *pyrrhic foot* (˘˘). It cannot provide the prevailing meter of a line.

Scansion, or marking stressed and unstressed syllables and then dividing the line into feet, is only approximate, for it seems to imply that all the stresses are equally heavy. Actually, a good reader will indicate a subtle variety of intensity in stresses in response to the sense of the lines. Here again are the first two lines of Christina Rossetti's "A Birthday":

> My heart | is like | a sing | ing bird
> Whose nest | is in | a wa | tered shoot.

Most readers will stress "heart" and "bird" more heavily than "like" and "sing," and "sing" more heavily than "like"; yet clearly even "like" is much more heavily stressed than any of the four unstressed syllables. For purposes of identifying the meter, all the stresses may be treated as equal; for purposes of reading aloud or determining the precise meaning of a line, the stressing must mediate between the ideal meter and the logical distribution of accents in the sentence. We can indicate one possible reading of a stanza quoted earlier by letting higher numbers indicate heavier stress:

> Out u | pon it! | I have | loved
> Three whole | days to | gether;
> And am | like to | love three | more,
> If it | prove fair | weather.

Thus the ideal meter is not wholly obliterated but is subtly modified by the logic of the phrases.

It is often useful to observe the length of lines in a given poem in terms of feet. Since the commonly used feet consist of one stressed syllable and one or two unstressed syllables, the number of feet will normally coincide with the number of stresses but will not have a constant relationship with the number of syllables. The terms used for line lengths are these: a one-foot line is called *monometer* (mo·nóm·e·tér); two-foot line, *dimeter* (dím·e·tér); three-foot line, *trimeter* (trím·e·tér); four-foot line, *tetrameter* (te·trám·e·tér); five-foot line, *pentameter* (pen·tám·e·tér); six-foot line, *hexameter* (hex·ám·e·tér). Longer lines are theoretically possible, but they are of such infrequent occurrence as to be of no concern here. In addition, they are usually best considered as a forcible joining of shorter lines so that what looks like heptameter may actually be an alternation of tetrameter and trimeter lines. These terms are joined with the names of feet to describe the ideal meter of various lines. Thus the meter of Blake's "The Tyger" is trochaic tetrameter, while the most frequent English line, used in sonnets, heroic couplets, blank verse, and a variety of other situations, is iambic pentameter.

Our examples have already shown that line lengths vary sometimes from the established length of the ideal meter. These variations are so irregular that most of the special vocabulary for such variations is of little value. One such change, though, is frequent enough to warrant some attention. Occasionally an iambic pentameter line will be extended by the addition of one extra foot to produce an *Alexandrine*. Spenser regularly uses such lines to conclude his characteristic stanzas, and they occur occasionally elsewhere. In the Spenserian stanza, the Alexandrine brings the stanza to rest, rounds it off, and concludes it. No such generalization covers other situations, though, for an Alexandrine may seem either accelerated or retarded in relation to the surrounding pentameter lines.

2. *Lines of Verse*

Another element in the rhythm of poetry is the natural pause within a line known as a *caesura*. In many lines the logic of phrasing produces a brief interruption along with a fall in pitch somewhere near the middle of the line:

A time there was, || ere England's griefs began.

In very long lines, as in the hexameter of *Evangeline*, secondary caesuras appear within the halves; indeed, any line longer than ten syllables tends to break into two parts, and in audible reading it will sound like two lines. The skillful poet finds in the caesura one more tool for shaping verse to his ends: he can enhance regularity by a precise placing of the caesura in the same place in each succeeding line, or he can give a loose, flowing, or informally conversational effect to his lines by varying the position of the caesura. Compare the practice of the following examples, assuming the position of the caesura to coincide with the internal mark of punctuation in each line:

> Be judge yourself, I'll bring it to the test,
> Which is the basest creature, man or beast:
> Birds feed on birds, beasts on each other prey;
> But savage man alone, does man betray.
> Pressed by necessity, *they* kill for food;
> Man undoes man, to do himself no good.
>
> .   .   .   .
> . . . Will share thy destiny. The gay will laugh
> When thou art gone, the solemn brood of care
> Plod on, and each one as before will chase
> His favorite phantom; yet all these shall leave
> Their mirth and their employments, and shall come
> And make their bed with thee. As the long train . . .

The reader can find clues to the significance of the lines or to an effective oral reading of them by observing the caesura position along with the other elements of form.

Lines may further be distinguished as *end stopped* or *run on*. The end-stopped line coincides with a logical unit of thought so that the line is usually ended by a mark of punctuation. The run-on (or *enjambed*) line contains a part of a unit of thought, or parts of two units of thought; the stops marked by punctuation are within the lines, or the thought units run through two or more lines, so that only a few of the lines are end stopped. Again, the poet can manipulate this feature of verse for a variety of effects. We cannot generalize in such a way as to account for all cases, but among the effects possible are a swiftly continuous argument or an easily flowing discourse produced by run-on lines as against a flatly oracular utterance produced by end-stopped lines. Notice that in the first example cited in the preceding paragraph all the lines are end stopped, whereas in the second example, all are run on. This quality, along with the difference in handling the caesura and along with the fact that the first example is rhymed and the second unrhymed, accounts for the striking differences in movement, tempo, and mood of these two iambic pentameter passages.

3. Stanza Forms

Finally, we should examine some of the ways in which lines are grouped to produce larger structural units.

Sometimes lines are irregularly grouped so that the divisions correspond to important stages in the development of the narrative or discussion. Such units vary in length and are not marked by any set scheme of rhymes, if, indeed, the lines are rhymed at all. These groupings are called *verse paragraphs*. They are likely to appear in long poems in *blank verse*—unrhymed iambic pentameter—and in *free verse*. Wordsworth's "Lines Composed a Few Miles above Tintern Abbey" provides a good example.

Groups of a definite number of lines, bound together by a *rhyme scheme* that reappears in each successive group, are called *stanzas*. (The term *verse* is sometimes incorrectly substituted for *stanza*. It should be reserved for its popular use in connection with songs, or to designate a single line of poetry.)

Pairs of two successive lines are called *couplets*. They are likely to be rhymed, or, if unrhymed, the second line of the couplet will be end stopped. Rhymed couplets may be *open*, that is, the second line will be run on so that the movement of the verse is free and continuous from one couplet to the next:

A thing of beauty is a joy forever;
Its loveliness increases; it will never
Pass into nothingness; but still will keep
A bower of quiet for us, and a sleep
Full of sweet dreams, and health, and quiet breathing.
Therefore, on every morrow, are we wreathing . . .

Closed couplets are self-contained. The first line is likely to be end stopped; the second line is sure to be. The effect is more formal and epigrammatic or more oracular than the free movement of open couplets:

True wit is nature to advantage dressed,
What oft was thought, but ne'er so well expressed;
Something, whose truth convinced at sight we find,
That gives us back the image of our mind.

Couplets are frequently written in iambic or trochaic tetrameter; in either meter they are often called *octosyllabic couplets* to call attention to the eight-syllable length of each line:

The lamb misused breeds public strife
And yet forgives the butcher's knife.
The bat that flits at close of eve
Has left the brain that won't believe.

Even more frequently, couplets are in iambic pentameter and are often called *decasyllabic couplets*. The closed decasyllabic couplet is sometimes known as a *heroic couplet*. This stanza, illustrated two paragraphs earlier, was used in the Restoration and eighteenth century, most notably by Dryden and Pope, for epic (heroic) or mock-heroic verse. It frequently showed a logical balance or antithesis pivoted about the caesura, or developed through the two lines of the couplet, and reinforced by alliteration and the rhyme:

Where wigs with wigs, with sword-knots sword-knots strive,
Beaux banish beaux, and coaches coaches drive.

It is still usual, by the way, to print couplets without stanza spacing, and some writers do not refer to couplets as stanzas, reserving this term for longer units set off by spacing.

Three successive rhyming lines as a variation in a sequence of heroic couplets are known as a *triplet*. In older printing practice, triplets were marked by a brace joining the three rhymes at the right end of the lines.

Three rhyming lines, of whatever length, handled as an independent stanza, form a *tercet*. Usually the three lines have the same rhyme, but other arrangements are possible if only two of the lines rhyme. An old development of the tercet, borrowed from Dante, is *terza rima,* iambic pentameter lines in which the first tercet rhymes *a b a.* The second tercet picks up the rhyme of the middle line in the first tercet so that its scheme is *b c b.* This pattern is repeated; the whole poem is tightly linked by its rhymes:

> As in that trance of wondrous thought I lay,
> This was the tenour of my waking dream:—
> Methought I sat beside a public way
>
> Thick with summer dust, and a great stream
> Of people there was hurrying to and fro,
> Numerous as gnats upon the evening gleam, . . .

Similar linking will appear also in the Spenserian stanza and the Spenserian sonnet.

A four-line stanza is known as a *quatrain*. Here some interesting variations are possible, not only because of the different line lengths and meters available, but also because the rhymes can be arranged in several ways. A common form rhymes *a b a b:*

> The curfew tolls the knell of parting day,
> The lowing herd wind slowly o'er the lea,
> The plowman homeward plods his weary way,
> And leaves the world to darkness and to me.

When the lines are of iambic pentameter, as they are here, the stanza is known as the *heroic* or *elegiac stanza*, the latter term from Gray's "Elegy Written in a Country Churchyard," from which we have quoted.

Some quatrains rhyme two lines only, thus: *x a x a*. One such quatrain is the *ballad stanza*, in which tetrameter and trimeter lines alternate:

> There lived a Wife at Usher's Well,
>   And a wealthy wife was she;
> She had three stout and stalwart sons,
>   And she sent them o'er the sea.

Note, by the way, that ballads are not always composed in this stanza form.

Another variation encloses the second rhyme within the first one: *a b b a*. This stanza is called an *envelope quatrain* or, if in iambic tetrameter, the *In Memoriam stanza*, from Tennyson's memorable use of it:

> Old Yew, which graspest at the stones
>   That name the under-lying dead,
>   Thy fibres net the dreamless head,
> Thy roots are wrapped about the bones.

An interesting special variety is the *Rubáiyát quatrain*, iambic pentameter lines rhyming *a a x a*:

> Awake! for Morning in the Bowl of Night
> Has flung the Stone that puts the Stars to Flight:
>   And Lo! the Hunter of the East has caught
> The Sultan's Turret in a Noose of Light.

Here the richness of the thrice-repeated rhyme is relieved by the unrhyming line, but enough similarity of line endings remains to make the quatrain tightly self-contained and to lend the quality of prophetic utterance to a "philosophic" poem.

Once we have passed four lines, the possible variations

in stanza form are too numerous to describe in detail, and
we add only the few stanza forms that have been used with
some frequency or that show some distinctive features. Of
the seven-line stanzas, *rime royal* is interesting because of
its effective use by Chaucer and some of his successors:

> Look how a tigress that hath lost her whelp
> Runs fiercely ranging through the woods astray,
> And seeing herself deprived of hope or help,
> Furiously assaults what's in her way,
> To satisfy her wrath, not for a prey;
>> So fell she on me in outrageous wise,
>> As could disdain and jealousy devise.

These are iambic pentameter lines rhyming *a b a b b c c*.
  Ottavarima consists of eight iambic pentameter lines
rhyming *a b a b a b c c*:

> He knew whose gentle hand was at the latch
>> Before the door had given her to his eyes;
> And from her chamber window he would catch
>> Her beauty farther than the falcon spies;
> And constant as her vespers would he watch,
>> Because her face was turned to the same skies;
> And with sick longing all the night outwear,
> To hear her morning step upon the stair.

This stanza requires a good bit of ingenuity in finding two
sets of three successive rhymes for each stanza (to say
nothing of the concluding couplet), but it has been used
with great success in long poems.
  One notable nine-line form is the *Spenserian stanza*,
devised by Spenser for *The Faerie Queene*, but also used
successfully by such later poets as Keats and Byron:

> Once more upon the waters! yet once more!
> And the waves bound beneath me as a steed
> That knows his rider. Welcome to their roar!
> Swift be their guidance, wheresoe'er it lead!
> Though the strained mast should quiver as a reed,

And the rent canvas fluttering strew the gale,
Still must I on; for I am as a weed,
Flung from the rock, on Ocean's foam to sail
Where'er the surge may sweep, the tempest's breath prevail.

The first eight lines are iambic pentameter; the ninth is iambic hexameter, or an Alexandrine. The prolongation of the final line combines with the closed rhyme of the couplet to bring the stanza to the repose of a definite conclusion. Another Spenserian trait, shown also in Spenser's personal variation on the English sonnet, is the linking of rhymes, in which the second rhyme of the first quatrain becomes the first rhyme of the second quatrain. Thus the rhyme scheme is *a b a b b c b c c.*

4. *The Sonnet*

We come now to what is perhaps the most esteemed stanza form, *the sonnet.* Its rather rigid rules have seemed a challenge to the poet to show how much range and variety he can create within the confines of its one hundred forty syllables, with the result that some of the most deftly fashioned poems in English, as well as many of the most intense and moving, take this form.

The term "sonnet" normally designates a lyric of fourteen iambic pentameter lines rhyming in one of several ways. Two basic forms, distinguished by their rhyme schemes and by their logical development, are frequent in English. The *Petrarchan* or *Italian sonnet* rhymes *a b b a, a b b a, c d e, c d e.* (The rhyming of the last six lines may vary; for example, *c d, c d, c d* is possible):

Divina Commedia, II

How strange the sculptures that adorn these towers!
This crowd of statues, in whose folded sleeves
Birds build their nests: while canopied with leaves
Parvis and portal bloom like trellised bowers,
And the vast minster seems a cross of flowers!
But fiends and dragons on the gargoyled eaves
Watch the dead Christ between the living thieves,

And, underneath, the traitor Judas lowers!
Ah! from what agonies of heart and brain,
What exultations trampling on despair,   10
What tenderness, what tears, what hate of wrong,
What passionate outcry of a soul in pain,
Uprose this poem of the earth and air,
This medieval miracle of song!

Such a sonnet tends to fall into two stages: the first eight
lines form the *octave*, and the last six the *sestet*. This
formal division is frequently reflected in the logical progress of the content. The octave will pose a problem, depict
a situation, or offer an observation. The sestet will provide
a resolution of this opening and bring the matter to a
conclusion, somewhat in the manner of a responsive reading in a church service.

A somewhat more widely used form is the *English* or
Shakespearean sonnet, which rhymes *a b a b, c d c d, e f e f,
g g*:

LXIV

When I have seen by Time's fell hand defaced
The rich proud cost of outworn buried age;
When sometime lofty towers I see down razed,
And brass eternal slave to mortal rage;
When I have seen the hungry ocean gain
Advantage on the kingdom of the shore,
And the firm soil win of the watery main,
Increasing store with loss, and loss with store;
When I have seen such interchange of state,
Or state itself confounded to decay,   10
Ruin hath taught me thus to ruminate,
That Time will come and take my love away.
This thought is as a death, which cannot choose
But weep to have that which it fears to lose.

Here the formal and logical divisions fall into three quatrains followed by a couplet. The quatrains will offer three
successive images, or experiences, or observations which

move by some rationale toward the resolution or conclusion of the couplet, which ends the sonnet much as Shakespeare's rhyming couplet marks the close of a blank-verse scene in the plays ("The play's the thing/Wherein I'll catch the conscience of the king."). Spenser's variation on the English sonnet, the *Spenserian sonnet*, a variation not much used by his successors, is a characteristic enhancing of the musical effect by linking rhymes to produce the scheme *a b a b, b c b c, c d c d, e e:*

Amoretti, LXXV

One day I wrote her name upon the strand,
But came the waves and washèd it away:
Agayne I wrote it with a second hand,
But came the tyde, and made my paynes his pray.
Vayne man, sayd she, that doest in vaine assay,
A mortall thing so to immortalize,
For I my selve shall lyke to this decay,
And eek my name bee wypèd out lykewize.
Not so, (quod I) let baser things devize
To dy in dust, but you shall live by fame: 10
My verse your vertues rare shall eternize,
And in the hevens wryte your glorious name.
Where whenas death shall all the world subdew,
Our love shall live, and later life renew.

While poets, as we have said, have been challenged by the strict form of the sonnet, they have also liked to experiment with it. A few sonneteers of the Renaissance used hexameter lines while observing all other conventions, whereas more recent poets have varied the number of lines. Thus Gerard Manley Hopkins produced what he called the "curtal" sonnet, curtailed to ten and a fraction lines. The sixteen-line poems of George Meredith's *Modern Love* are sometimes called sonnets because their logical development is much the same as that of the standard sonnet. Undoubtedly the possibilities of this noble form have not been exhausted.

5. *Free Verse*

Before leaving our consideration of versification, we should note the vigorous unorthodoxy of *free verse*. In this style, brought to full development only during the past century, the poet rejects all predetermined meters and stanzaic structures on the grounds that they are molds into which his ideas must be poured. He maintains that the ideas have a form implicit within them which will sprout, branch, and flower as the poem grows. This theory of *organic form* produces poetry which looks on the page quite unlike any regular poetry, for both its lines and its verse paragraphs are of widely varying lengths. In addition, such poetry is unrhymed and does not conform to any ideal meter. Yet free verse is not simply prose chopped up into arbitrary line lengths. Its diction, its liberal use of figurative language and of symbols, and its essentially dramatic method all mark it as belonging to the great tradition of poetry. As verse, it is considerably more rhythmic than prose, tending to fall into iambic patterns which coincide with the logical rhythms of the phrases so that there is a pulse in the lines that reinforces the sense of the sentences. Similarly, the contours of the verse paragraphs parallel the development of the thought. In Walt Whitman's poetry, the typical verse paragraph begins with lines of moderate length, proceeds through lines of increasing length to a climax, and concludes with lines of decreasing length:

> Have you reckon'd a thousand acres much? have you
>   reckon'd the earth much?
> Have you practis'd so long to learn to read?
> Have you felt so proud to get at the meaning of poems?
> Stop this day and night with me and you shall possess
>   the origin of all poems,
> You shall possess the good of the earth and sun, (there
>   are millions of suns left,)

You shall no longer take things at second or third hand,
    nor look through the eyes of the dead, nor feed on
    the spectres in books,
You shall not look through my eyes either, nor take things
    from me,
You shall listen to all sides and filter them from your self.

The effect is something like that of a wave gathering strength, cresting, and subsiding. Clearly no rules of scansion or stanza analysis will apply to free verse; we must deal with each example on its own terms to discover how its highly individual metric effects contribute to the whole poem.

C. Form and Meaning

This observation brings us to the most important phase of our discussion of poetic form. An understanding of meters and their relationship to rhythm, of rhyme schemes and sound values, of stanza forms and strategies of organization is essential to the full apprehension and appreciation of poetry, but it is only preliminary to our realization of the total effect of poetic form. From time to time we have suggested that one device or another may have a given effect; actually the effect of any stratagem may be judged only in its total setting, and there the result may be slightly to wholly different from its usual effect. The practice of judging effects may seem subjective or vaguely impressionistic. Actually it is based on a solid knowledge of the techniques that we have been describing, but it also proceeds by the application of this knowledge through sensitivity and imagination.

A few examples will suggest how one can move from technical analysis to the judging of effects. Alexander Pope is now generally acknowledged to be one of the great masters of the manipulation of verse techniques. Beyond this, he has been very useful to commentators on poetry, for *An Essay on Criticism* not only states but also ingeniously illustrates some of the ways a poet can match the sound to sense. In a famous passage, Pope belabors several kinds of inept critics as well as the poetry they admire and imitates bad verse in such lines as "Though oft the ear the open vowels tire" or "And ten low words oft creep in one dull line." Then, after telling us that "The sound must seem an echo to the sense," he produces these remarkable lines:

> Soft is the strain when Zephyr gently blows,
> And the smooth stream in smoother numbers flows;
> But when loud surges lash the sounding shore,
> The hoarse, rough verse should like the torrent roar:
> When Ajax strives some rock's vast weight to throw,
> The line too labours, and the words move slow;
> Not so, when swift Camilla scours the plain,
> Flies o'er th' unbending corn, and skims along the main.

How has Pope managed this ingenious adjustment of verse technique and meaning? Note, first, that he has achieved great variety within the limits of the closed couplet. All the lines are end stopped, and each couplet concludes with a mark of punctuation indicating a full or nearly full stop. Obviously the variety is produced by techniques operating within the essentially uniform couplets.

In the first two lines (as indeed throughout the passage) we are struck by a rather heavy use of alliteration: the *s* sounds through "*s*oft," "i*s*," "*s*train," "blow*s*," "*s*mooth," "*s*tream," "*s*moother," "number*s*," and "flow*s*." In addition, the Z of "Zephyr" and even the *g* of "gently" are nearly enough related to the *s* sound to reinforce it. This sequence of alliteration is interlinked with a second sequence playing on *n* and *m*: "strai*n*," "whe*n*," "ge*n*tly," "a*n*d," "s*m*ooth," "strea*m*," "s*m*oother," and "*n*u*m*bers." "Soft" and "smooth" are terms that justly characterize these sounds.

We might also examine the meter of these lines to see

how the distribution of stresses contributes to the effects generated by alliteration:

> Sóft ĭs | thĕ stráin | whĕn Zéph | y̆r gént | ly̆ blóws,
> Ănd thĕ | smóoth stréam | ĭn smóoth | ĕr núm | bĕrs
>   flóws; . . .

In the first line a trochee is substituted for the opening iamb; in the second line the stress is shifted from its normal position in the second syllable to the third syllable. Both of these variations bring two unstressed syllables together early in the line, with the effect of a light skipping step. Thereafter both lines are smoothly regular in harmony with the smooth effect of the alliterative sequences. This analysis does not exhaust the possibilities of the two lines, but it suggests some of the devices at work.

The next couplet offers a sharp contrast to the first, as the transitional word "but" indicates. If we look again at alliteration, we find once more a good many s sounds: "surges," "sounding," "hoarse," "verse." How is this? Can the same sound in one line product soft, smooth effects and in the next line create hoarse, hissing sounds? Well, yes it can, depending on the other devices it is associated with, and on the meanings—the denotations and connotations—of the words. This time one alliterative sequence plays on sh: "lash," "shore," "should"; these words produce a harsh sound. But this is not really fair, for in another situation we might find ourselves contending that sh produces a muffled, hushed effect; furthermore, the l of "loud," "lash," and "like" is not inherently rough. As for the surrounding sounds not included in the alliterating sequences, the second couplet is only a very little harsher than the first. Two conclusions are in order here: First, a small difference in sound quality may be very important. Second, we reiterate that our perception of the emotional qualities of sounds is conditioned by the meanings of the words that carry the sounds.

The distribution of stresses in the second couplet may also contribute to the rougher effect of those lines:

But when | loud sur | ges lash | the sound | ing shore,

The hoarse, | rough verse | should like | the tor | rent

     roar: . .

Here we have indicated six stresses in the first line. Normally the third syllable of each line would be unstressed, but the natural rhythm of the words simply will not permit us to read these syllables as unstressed. This natural rhythm is, of course, a product of the meaning of the words.

The third couplet presents still another kind of peculiarity. Again we find a number of *s* sounds piling up in the first half of the first line, but this time we are affected not so much by any inherent imitative quality in the sounds themselves as by the fact that the *s*'s are so arranged that they are difficult to pronounce. The *s* sound at the end of "Ajax" is immediately followed by the initial *s* of "strives"; again, the juncture of "strives" and "some" presents the same impediment, and the juxtaposition of "weight" and "to" later in the line uses *t*'s for this effect. Indeed, throughout the four couplets we are examining, the tempo, smoothness, and emotional quality of the lines are all influenced by the ease or difficulty of pronouncing the combinations of sounds and stresses. In the first line of this third couplet, Pope uses no unusual metrical effects, but the second line stretches the iambic to its utmost:

The line | too la | bours, and | the words | move slow; . . .

A further quality involved here is syllable weight. Some syllables are simply bulkier than others; they cannot be pronounced rapidly or lightly. Here Pope has piled up three heavy syllables: "words," "move," "slow," with virtually equal stresses, in a sequence that is reminiscent of "And ten low words oft creep in one dull line."

Certainly the last couplet of the Pope passage moves swiftly. The meter of the first line is perfectly regular, the syllables are light, and there are no combinations of sounds that are difficult to pronounce. The last line, though, is metrically unusual; it is an Alexandrine, since it contains twelve syllables, as against the usual ten for an iambic pentameter line. (The fusion of "th'" and "un-" produces a single syllable: "th'un.") A few lines above, Pope has accused clumsy poets of marring their verse by tossing in limping Alexandrines—and he has proved his point by producing a very slow line indeed:

A needless Alexandrine ends the song,
That, like a wounded snake, drags its slow length along.

The resolution of the apparent discrepancy between the usual weighty slowness of the Alexandrine and its swiftness in this situation lies in the different *combinations* of qualities that Pope has used in the two lines. Thus we must be very cautious in putting forward generalizations about the effect of any single aspect of verse viewed in isolation and must examine all the aspects of poetry as they work together.

Now, this has been a long and detailed analysis of a few lines. We shall not want to linger over every poem in this way, but the ability to comprehend poetry fairly readily without laborious metrical analysis is a skill developed by patient apprenticeship in the art of analysis.

Finally, though, the most important point is this: the analysis of poetic form is not an end in itself. There is not much value in determining that a stanza is an iambic tetrameter quatrain rhyming *a b b a*, or that the poet has used alliteration of certain sounds, or that he has used this or that figure of speech if we do not go on to assemble these separate observations into some kind of comprehensive account of the poem. To do that we must consider certain aspects of the content of poems.

IV

The Content of Poetry

A. Narrative

We said some distance back that poetry usually has a *narrative* element, which may be either the main concern in the poem or subordinate to the treatment of an emotion, idea, or character portrait. Only two problems—neither of them very difficult—present themselves here. The first is simply the matter of tracing out the story. In many narrative poems we shall have no difficulty at all. The story will be told in a straightforward manner, with a full array of expository statements to make things just as clear as possible, as it is in many ballads, Scott's long narratives such as "The Lady of the Lake," Longfellow's "The Courtship of Miles Standish," Tennyson's *Idylls of the King*, Jeffers's "The Roan Stallion," and, indeed, most other narrative poems. As a general rule, if the narrative is not immediately clear, we should examine the nature and source of the obscurity to determine its effect. What we are really trying to find out, of course, is why the poet somewhat veiled his story. We cannot interview the poet about his intention nor expect him to give a complete answer if we could, but we can determine the effect of what he does. It is possible that the story is made more vivid by dramatization and consists only of dialogue. In such a situation the reader becomes an active participant in creating the setting of the poem. Sometimes the reader's imagination is stimulated by unspecified joys or horrors as it could not be by precise detail. Occasionally the poet will tell his story in a roundabout manner so that the poem's significance is more powerful when it occurs to the reader, just as an explosive produces more damage when it is tightly confined. In the following sonnet by Edwin Arlington Robinson, reconstruct what happened by seeking answers to these questions: Why is the entire poem enclosed in quotation marks? What is the dramatic situation of the poem? How accurately does the speaker describe himself in line 3? Why does he refer to Annandale in line 1 as "it"? What does he mean in line 13 by "a slight kind of engine"? What is he doing as he says, "Do you see?/Like this . . . "? What does the title mean?

How Annandale Went Out

"They called it Annandale—and I was there
To flourish, to find words, and to attend:
Liar, physician, hypocrite, and friend,
I watched him; and the sight was not so fair
As one or two that I had seen elsewhere:
An apparatus not for me to mend—
A wreck, with hell between him and the end,
Remained of Annandale; and I was there.
I knew the ruin as I knew the man;
So put the two together, if you can,   10
Remembering the worst you know of me.
Now view yourself as I was, on the spot—
With a slight kind of engine. Do you see?
Like this. . . . You wouldn't hang me? I thought not."

When you feel that you have satisfactorily reconstructed the story in the poem, consider the effect of this veiled presentation. Would the poem have been as effective if Robinson had told it in a straightforward, immediately clear manner? This kind of indirect narration is rare, though, and we need not plague ourselves about "hidden meanings"; generally, poets labor to make their meaning clear, and we find difficulties only because there is so much meaning to be found in a brief work.

The second problem is to discover whether the narrative is central or only tributary to another matter. The poems named at the beginning of this section seem to be concerned primarily with telling an exciting or moving story, as we deduce from the prominence given to action for its own sake. Some narratives, though, use action and speech chiefly as means of character revelation, as do the dramatic monologues of Robert Browning or such narratives of Frost as "The Death of the Hired Man." Others use narrative to dramatize ideas. "Ozymandias" is one brief example; a more fully elaborated one is Robinson's "The Man Against the Sky." Autobiographical poems may deal with the growth and nature of the poet's vocation. Two such different poems as Wordsworth's "The Prelude" and Whitman's "Out of the Cradle Endlessly Rocking" use narrative to this end. Epics such as *Beowulf* and *Paradise Lost* deal by narrative means with such large themes as the origins and ideals of a people or the vindication of God's ways. Finally, almost all lyrics use an incident, however simple, to provide the occasion for the poet's emotion and the means of expressing it. If there is any need to determine the relative importance of narrative and other elements, some well-established criteria can be applied. What portion of the space in the poem is given to the story? What devices of emphasis such as vivid wording, emphatic phrasing, or climactic position are given to the story as against the meditation or character portrait? Actually, we are only trying to decide where the chief weight of the poem lies, for narrative, emotion, and idea are likely to help each other along and may actually be inseparable. Poems are not often versified philosophical treatises, and in some sense, at least, the ideas they convey are realizable only in the context of a given experience.

B. Emotion

One of the characteristics that distinguish literature from nonliterary writing is its concern with conveying the emotion that accompanies an experience, and of all the literary forms poetry deals with emotion most ably. The very large body of poetry concerned primarily with expressing emotion is called *lyric poetry*. Emotion can be conveyed in many ways: the connotations of the diction, the lilt or drag of the rhythms, the associations surrounding the images, the significance of the events narrated—all these elements cooperate to establish the emotion. Hence the reader's experience, learning, and sensitivity are all necessary to help detect the emotional quality of a poem. Sometimes, it is true, a poet will declare his emotion by naming it, by saying that he experiences it. A famous example is Shelley's "The Indian Serenade":

The Indian Serenade

I arise from dreams of thee
In the first sweet sleep of night,
When the winds are breathing low,
And the stars are shining bright:
I arise from dreams of thee,
And a spirit in my feet
Hath led me—who knows how?
To thy chamber window, Sweet!

The wandering airs they faint
On the dark, the silent stream—   10
The Champak odours fail
Like sweet thoughts in a dream;
The nightingale's complaint,
It dies upon her heart;—
As I must on thine,
Oh, beloved as thou art!

Oh lift me from the grass!
I die! I faint! I fail!

Let thy love in kisses rain
On my lips and eyelids pale. 20
My cheek is cold and white, alas!
My heart beats loud and fast;—
Oh! press it to thine own again,
Where it will break at last.

In judging the effectiveness of "The Indian Serenade," we must decide whether the imagery and narrative are of the right kind and intensity to elicit in the reader the emotion proclaimed by the poet. Modern critics are inclined to distrust the efficacy of this method of communicating emotion, and indeed T. S. Eliot, one of the most influential of recent critics as well as a distinguished poet, has insisted that art can convey emotion only by presenting what he calls an "objective correlative"—an object, an action, a situation which is the "formula" of that particular emotion and which, when presented to the reader, produces a sense impression that elicits the emotion. This idea implies a widely or universally shared response to particular objects and situations. Presumably what aroused the emotion in the poet can be counted on to evoke it in the reader as well. Such a concept will serve if we understand that the formal aspects of poetry—sound values, diction, and structure, for example—may be included among objective correlatives. The following sonnet by Wordsworth opens with a declaration of emotion by saying directly that the scene to be pictured is "A sight . . . touching in its majesty." The imagery that follows fully justifies the claim, and might indeed stand alone without the expository opening:

Composed upon Westminster Bridge

Sept. 3, 1802

Earth has not anything to show more fair:
Dull would he be of soul who could pass by
A sight so touching in its majesty:
This city now doth, like a garment, wear

The beauty of the morning; silent, bare,
Ships, towers, domes, theatres, and temples lie
Open unto the fields, and to the sky;
All bright and glittering in the smokeless air.
Never did sun more beautifully steep
In his first splendour, valley, rock, or hill;   10
Ne'er saw I, never felt, a calm so deep!
The river glideth at his own sweet will:
Dear God! the very houses seem asleep;
And all that mighty heart is lying still!

A special aspect of emotion is the *tone* of a literary work, which may be defined as the attitude of the author toward his subject matter as it reveals itself in the literary work. Ordinarily the reader will have to draw inferences from the diction, the sound effects, the figures, and the ideas of the poem. Light, jingling rhythms imply one attitude, and sonorous, stately measures another. Laudatory epithets probably suggest the author's esteem while grotesque appellations or comparisons may show his contempt for a character. In "Holy Thursday" William Blake uses a series of rhetorical questions to make clear his indignation at social injustices:

Holy Thursday

Is this a holy thing to see
In a rich and fruitful land,
Babes reduced to misery,
Fed with cold and usurous hand?

Is that trembling cry a song?
Can it be a song of joy?
And so many children poor?
It is a land of poverty!

And their sun does never shine,
And their fields are bleak and bare,   10
And their ways are filled with thorns:
It is eternal winter there.

> For where'er the sun does shine,
> And where'er the rain does fall,
> Babe can never hunger there,
> Nor poverty the mind appall.

Two pitfalls need to be avoided here. First, we must be sure whether an attitude is to be attributed to the poet or to a character. In Browning's dramatic monologues, the views of the fictional speaker are often overtly expressed, or fairly clearly implied; the attitudes of the poet must be deduced from the gradually revealed portrait of the speaker:

My Last Duchess

FERRARA

That's my last Duchess painted on the wall,
Looking as if she were alive; I call
That piece a wonder, now: Frà Pandolf's hands
Worked busily a day, and there she stands.
Will't please you sit and look at her? I said
"Frà Pandolf" by design, for never read
Strangers like you that pictured countenance,
The depth and passion of its earnest glance,
But to myself they turned (since none puts by
The curtain I have drawn for you, but I)   10
And seemed as they would ask me, if they durst,
How such a glance came there; so, not the first
Are you to turn and ask thus. Sir, 'twas not
Her husband's presence only, called that spot
Of joy into the Duchess' cheek: perhaps
Frà Pandolf chanced to say "Her mantle laps
Over my Lady's wrist too much," or "Paint
Must never hope to reproduce the faint
Half-flush that dies along her throat,": such stuff
Was courtesy, she thought, and cause enough   20
For calling up that spot of joy. She had
A heart—how shall I say?—too soon made glad,
Too easily impressed; she liked whate'er
She looked on, and her looks went everywhere.
Sir, 'twas all one! My favour at her breast,

The dropping of the daylight in the West.
The bough of cherries some officious fool
Broke in the orchard for her, the white mule
She rode with round the terrace—all and each
Would draw from her alike the approving speech,   30
Or blush, at least. She thanked men,—good; but thanked
Somehow—I know not how—as if she ranked
My gift of a nine-hundred-years-old name
With anybody's gift. Who'd stoop to blame
This sort of trifling? Even had you skill
In speech—(which I have not)—to make your will
Quite clear to such an one, and say, "Just this
Or that in you disgusts me; here you miss,
Or there exceed the mark"—and if she let
Herself be lessoned so, nor plainly set   40
Her wits to yours, forsooth, and made excuse,
—E'en then would be some stooping, and I choose
Never to stoop. Oh, Sir, she smiled, no doubt,
Whene'er I passed her; but who passed without
Much the same smile? This grew; I gave commands;
Then all smiles stopped together. There she stands
As if alive. Will't please you rise? We'll meet
The company below, then. I repeat,
The Count your Master's known munificence
Is ample warrant that no just pretence   50
Of mine for dowry will be disallowed;
Though his fair daughter's self, as I avowed
At starting, is my object. Nay, we'll go
Together down, Sir! Notice Neptune, though,
Taming a sea-horse, thought a rarity,
Which Claus of Innsbruck cast in bronze for me.

Second, we must be alert for irony as a key to tone.
Arthur Hugh Clough's irony in "The Latest Decalogue"
conveys a tone of condemnation toward modern hypocrisy:

The Latest Decalogue

Thou shalt have one God only; who
Would be at the expense of two?
No graven images may be
Worshipped, except the currency:

Swear not at all; for, for thy curse
Thine enemy is none the worse:
At church on Sunday to attend
Will serve to keep the world thy friend:
Honour thy parents; that is, all
From whom advancement may befall: 10
Thou shalt not kill; but need'st not strive
Officiously to keep alive:
Do not adultery commit;
Advantage rarely comes of it:
Thou shalt not steal; an empty feat,
When 'tis so lucrative to cheat:
Bear not false witness; let the lie
Have time on its own wings to fly:
Thou shalt not covet, but tradition
Approves all forms of competition.   20

For another example, the ironic inscription in "Ozymandias" establishes the tone of the whole sonnet; that is, it shows us Shelley's attitude toward his subject.

C. Ideas

We have already said that poems are not versified philosophy, and, in repeatedly insisting that the poem is a unified whole that should be dissected only as a means toward realizing its wholeness, we have implied that the idea, or theme, or meaning of a poem is not a separable part that can be better understood after the clutter of versification or metaphor is stripped away. The ideas of poems are important, though, and poets give memorable embodiment to ideas or, better, provide a rich sensuous, emotional, and intellectual realization of a theme which no purely rational process could provide.

1. Historical Context

One important clue to the pattern of ideas in a poem is its date. In successive periods of history certain dominant climates of belief prevail; in fact, we may define periods of history partly by identifying their dominant outlooks so that we are able to speak of "the Age of Faith," or "the Age of Reason," or "the Age of Skepticism." Certainly not everyone will accept the majority view in a given period, but we can usually relate a particular poem to the dominant views of its time.

A few examples will help clarify this matter; suppose we concentrate for the moment on the nature of the Deity. Poets, like all imaginative writers, are concerned ultimately with the human condition; it matters greatly to them, then, whether the world as we know it was created by some intelligent Force or just happened as the result of a series of undesigned unique accidents. If it was created by an intelligent Force, then in turn it matters greatly whether that Force is an eternal, fatherly God or a vast impersonal power indifferent to man, perhaps no longer active. Mankind, through its long history, has examined an amazing variety of solutions to these problems, and the poets have given voice to them.

One aspect of the Romanticism that arose late in the eighteenth century and flowered in the early nineteenth century was an image of the Deity as a spirit interfused in all things, as Wordsworth suggests in "Tintern Abbey":

> And I have felt
> A presence that disturbs me with the joy
> Of elevated thoughts; a sense sublime
> Of something far more deeply interfused,
> Whose dwelling is the light of setting suns,
> And the round ocean and the living air,
> And the blue sky, and in the mind of man:
> A motion and a spirit, that impels
> All thinking things, all objects of all thought,
> And rolls through all things.

In contrast to Wordsworth's living universe is Edwin Arlington Robinson's picture of a dead, meaningless universe that offers no moral guidance. Even here the poet

finds hope, but his "Credo" ("I believe") is a testament
of faith—of belief, that is, without evidence:

Credo

I cannot find my way: there is no star
In all the shrouded heavens anywhere;
And there is not a whisper in the air
Of any living voice but one so far
That I can hear it only as a bar
Of lost, imperial music, played when fair
And angel fingers wove, and unaware,
Dead leaves to garlands where no roses are.
No, there is not a glimmer, nor a call,
For one that welcomes, welcomes when he fears,   10
The black and awful chaos of the night;
For through it all—above, beyond it all—
I know the far-sent message of the years,
I feel the coming glory of the Light.

The date of Robinson's poem, about 1894, is hardly necessary to tell us that he is echoing the troubled doubt of a
modern world struggling to reconcile traditional faith and
new skepticism.

If there are certain ways of perceiving things characteristic of a particular age, there are also ideas that persist or
reappear from time to time through history. The Wordsworth passage from "Tintern Abbey," for example, reflects
the idea that the Soul of the Universe flows through and
encompasses all things, including "the mind of man." In
this view all individual souls are parts of one great Oversoul and are either temporarily or incompletely separated
from it. While separated they are in a fallen and imperfect
condition, and their intensely desired destiny is to be re-
united with the Oversoul, and hence with each other.
Thus ultimately all mankind would achieve a reunion in
which painful individual identities would be merged in the
great Soul which is God. This idea is not restricted to any
single period of history but has formed part of the world
view of various cultures that have borrowed it from older

eras and added their own modifications. It occurs in both Hindu and Neo-Platonic philosophy and reappears in the English metaphysical poets of the seventeenth century and in German, English, and American romantic philosophy in the nineteenth century. Here is a seventeenth-century expression of the idea from "The Waterfall" by Henry Vaughan:

> Dear stream! dear bank, where often I
> Have sat and pleased my pensive eye,
> Why, since each drop of thy quick store
> Runs thither whence it flowed before,
> Should poor souls fear a shade or night,
> Who came, sure, from a sea of light?
> Or since those drops are all sent back
> So sure to thee, that none doth lack,
> Why should frail flesh doubt any more
> That what God takes he'll not restore?

The following poem shows a late nineteenth-century version of the idea by an American Romantic, Ralph Waldo Emerson:

Pan

> O what are heroes, prophets, men,
> But pipes through which the breath of Pan doth blow
> A momentary music. Being's tide
> Swells hitherward, and myriads of forms
> Live, robed with beauty, painted by the sun;
> Their dust, pervaded by the nerves of God,
> Throbs with an overmastering energy
> Knowing and doing. Ebbs the tide, they lie
> White hollow shells upon the desert shore,
> But not the less the eternal wave rolls on   10
> To animate new millions, and exhale
> Races and planets, its enchanted foam.

In these examples, the Oversoul is pictured as water—a stream, or the sea—a great reservoir of which each individual soul is an inlet, or from which it is separated as a drop, a current, or a tidal pool.

2. *Explicit Statement versus Metaphor*

By what means have the ideas in our examples been conveyed? The quotation from Wordsworth proceeds largely by explicit statement. In a perfectly direct way the poet makes an essentially expository statement, bringing to his aid little more than the resources of versification. Several of the important nouns are abstract: "Presence," "something," "motion," "spirit," "things"; only the barest hint of personification or metaphor appears in "interfused," "dwelling," "impels," "rolls." In our insistence upon the concrete and dramatic quality of poetry, we may seem to have implied that there is no place in it for explicit, literal statement. Actually there is, but it is a minor place; the characteristic method of poetic statement is dramatic and figurative. The essence of figurative language is doubleness. Such figures as metaphor, simile, metonymy, synecdoche, and personification, and the rhetorical devices of ambiguity—the pun, paradox, oxymoron, and verbal irony —all involve the linking of two things. Thus the poet attends simultaneously to the concrete and the abstract, the literal and the figurative, the near at hand and the absent or intangible. Our quotations from Vaughan and Emerson proceed largely by metaphor; some equivalence is asserted so that the idea stated abstractly by Wordsworth can be handled in terms of some visible, palpable objects, some of whose qualities are shared by the abstraction. Though by no means superior to the Wordsworth extract as poetry, they do use the commoner, more characteristic method of indirection.

3. *Allegory*

When a metaphor is much extended, and especially when the poet develops a narrative out of a complex of subordinate metaphors derived from the main one, we designate the result *allegory*. In an earlier section we examined Ralegh's "What Is Our Life?" as an example of extended metaphor. That ingenious little poem falls short of allegory only by a lack of narrative. Matthew Arnold's "To Marguerite" is clearly also an extended metaphor, but, since it contains a stronger narrative element than the Ralegh poem, it is closer to allegory:

To Marguerite

Yes! in the sea of life enisled,
With echoing straits between us thrown,
Dotting the shoreless watery wild,
We mortal millions live *alone*.
The islands feel the enclasping flow,
And then their endless bounds they know.

But when the moon their hollows lights,
And they are swept by balms of spring,
And in their glens, on starry nights,
The nightingales divinely sing;   10
And lovely notes, from shore to shore,
Across the sounds and channels pour—

Oh! then a longing like despair
Is to their farthest caverns sent;
For surely once, they feel, we were
Parts of a single continent!
Now round us spreads the watery plain—
Oh might our marges meet again!

Who order'd, that their longing's fire
Should be, as soon as kindled, cool'd?   20
Who renders vain their deep desire?—
A God, a God their severance ruled!
And bade betwixt their shores to be
The unplumb'd, salt, estranging sea.

The opening lines establish the main metaphor of which all the others are parts: life is represented by a sea. The human race is represented by islands separated by the "unplumb'd, salt, estranging sea." (Compare this idea with John Donne's "No man is an island.") Our moments of joy are balmy spring nights. Our intermittent communications are the distant songs of nightingales. In our original united condition we were an unbroken continent.

What qualities of this poem mark it as allegorical? First, it is a fabric of consistently related metaphors connected into a narrative. The secondary terms of these metaphors —the concrete, literal objects (sea; islands) that stand for abstract or undepicted things (life; human begins)—are called *allegorical signs*. Second, the relationship between each allegorical sign and the thing it signifies is arbitrary: islands bear no very close actual resemblance to men; there is no natural relationship between them. Third, each of the allegorical signs has but a single significance, even though a number of them (moon; balms of spring; nightingales) evoke a cluster of emotions. Allegory, even though highly elaborated into a very long narrative furnished with many characters and incidents as in *The Faerie Queene*, still retains these characteristics.

4. Symbol

Still another way of embodying an idea is by means of the *symbol*. In the broadest usage, a symbol is any thing that stands for something else. In this very general sense any thing which is of interest chiefly to the extent that it represents some single, uncomplicated idea can be called a symbol, so that the term sometimes includes allegorical signs, all words, red lights that signify "stop," or asterisks that indicate "Look at the bottom of the page." Actually such things are more properly designated *signs*. The term "symbol" can then be reserved for an object, an action, a situation, a verbal formula that represents the complexity of an abstraction, an unseen object, an unfamiliar object, any phenomenon so vast or complex that it cannot be dealt with directly or literally—or several of these at once. The symbol will usually evoke the emotions that surround the symbolized thing, and it will in various contexts suggest varying aspects of the thing represented. In addition, the symbol will have some kind of natural relationship to the thing it stands for. It can be a representative example of a large group of things so that, for example, a particular soldier might symbolize all fighting men. It can embody many characteristics of the thing symbolized: the rose as a symbol of beauty is itself beautful, but it is also fragile, transient, and without utility; a circle may symbolize wholeness or unity, for it is itself whole and unified. It can be closely associated with the history of what it symbolizes; the cross was the object actually used for the crucifixion of Christ, and it has come to symbolize all things related to Christianity, not only the suffering of Christ, but also the history of the religion, the company of believers, and the doctrines of Christianity. (The cross may also be used as a sign to mark a church building, either in actuality or on a map; in the form of a lapel button it may be a sign identifying a Christian. Though thus used as a sign, it may also still operate as a symbol to the extent that it represents the complex, unseen things we have listed.) Finally, the symbol usually stands for several things, which may or may not be related. While we can identify the several referents of the symbol, we cannot wholly elucidate its complex meaning, so that to an extent the symbol is the only way of expressing what it symbolizes.

Clearly the symbol, like the allegorical sign, is a kind of metaphor in associating two things generally unlike each other but sharing a number of important qualities. The symbol, as it appears in literature, usually stands for a thing unnamed. The question becomes, then, how we know that an object, an action, a situation, or a verbal formula is a symbol, and how we know what it stands for. There has been a vast amount of quarreling over these questions in recent years among professional critics, so that the student need not grieve if he misses symbolic meanings or if he does not always agree with interpretations that are offered to him. Actually the disagreements of the critics are more spectacular and amusing than their agreements, so that the quarrels obscure the large areas of generally accepted theory and the large body of settled interpretation. One man's guess is not as good as another's, but we are dealing with a complex and difficult matter that in the nature of things can never be reduced to an exact science. There are some guides, though, that we can use to get us started toward the inquisitive ingenuity of the practiced reader of poetry.

First, many objects have been used for so long and so consistently as symbols that we do well to be alert to symbolic possibilities wherever they occur. Roads, streams, and journeys of all kinds have been likened to life in both metaphor and symbol so often that it takes a really inventive mind to use such a symbol effectively. Yet great writers repeatedly manage such a feat. The sea is sometimes used to represent the source of life, or life itself, or death, or the unconscious. The passage of day and night, or the progress of the seasons can represent the transience of human life. William Blake's "The Lamb" not only uses traditional associations of gentleness and innocence, but also reminds us that the lamb is a symbol of Christ. All these things may become *public symbols*, for they are the common possession of most literate beings; they have been used by most nations and throughout history. Authors may also use *nonce* or *private symbols*, which occur uniquely in a single literary work, or only in their collected works, as William Butler Yeats uses the city of Byzantium to symbolize an ideal alternative to the actual, modern world. Sometimes it is necessary to discover the significance of a symbol from sources outside the work itself, such as autobiographies, letters, or prose works like Yeats's *A Vision*, but this necessity is really very rare. The work under examination will ordinarily tell us what we need to know. Sometimes the poet tells us what his symbol means, as Whitman does when he refers to his locomotive as "type of the modern." Even without such help, we recognize that William Blake in "The Tyger" uses a powerful and terrifying animal to represent all the malevolent forces of the universe. Thus the line, "Did he who made the

Lamb make thee?" asks whether the God who created the goodness of Christ also created evil.

The Tyger

Tyger! Tyger! burning bright
In the forests of the night,
What immortal hand or eye
Could frame thy fearful symmetry?

In what distant deeps or skies
Burnt the fire of thine eyes?
On what wings dare he aspire?
What the hand dare seize the fire?

And what shoulder, and what art,
Could twist the sinews of thy heart?   10
And when thy heart began to beat,
What dread hand? and what dread feet?

What the hammer? what the chain?
In what furnace was thy brain?
What the anvil? what dread grasp
Dare its deadly terrors clasp?

When the stars threw down their spears,
And watered heaven with their tears,
Did he smile his work to see?
Did he who made the Lamb make thee?   20

Tyger! Tyger! burning bright
In the forests of the night,
What immortal hand or eye,
Dare frame thy fearful symmetry?

If an object is given great prominence as by repetition at crucial points, we should suspect that it carries symbolic meaning. This observation is especially true if no other purpose can be attributed to the object. Good writers write less casually than they may seem to do; everything in a work is directed to some end. A difficulty here is that the truly effective literary artist usually accomplishes several things with each move he makes. A well-assimilated symbol, then, will also advance the literal narrative, or create valuable atmosphere, and will probably not cry out for symbolic interpretation to justify its existence.

The final test of an interpretation of a piece of symbolism is that it legitimately illuminates the work. By "legitimately" we mean that the interpretation is founded solidly on evidence in the work and is not a ramshackle remodeling of the original structure hanging over the void without a foundation. A sound interpretation carries conviction with it; it comports with good sense; it accounts for everything in the poem and requires nothing which is not either in the poem or clearly relevant to it.*

5. *Allusion*

Another aspect of the content of poems is *allusion*, which may be defined as reference, without lengthy explanation, to literature, history, or current events. In these few lines of Emerson, we should recognize allusions by means of paraphrase to the proverbial expression "poor but proud," to the Declaration of Independence ("men are endowed by their Creator with certain unalienable rights"), and to "America" ("Long may our land be bright/With freedom's holy light"):

---

* Published discussion of allegory and symbolism is extensive, inconsistent, and confusing. Rather than present all the alternative definitions and descriptions of these vexed terms, we have taken a particular position which we believe to be consistent and clear without a proliferation of sub-classes to cover all examples. A glance at some of the alternatives rejected here may be useful.

Our definition of allegory extends its terrain considerably beyond the limits usually fixed for it. It is customary to say that the allegorist invents an artificial world as a means of teaching a moral lesson applicable to the actual world. The characters are personified qualities bearing appropriate names (Fidelity; Duessa) or representative types appropriately

I am not poor, but I am proud,
  Of one inalienable right,
Above the envy of the crowd,—
  Thought's holy light.

Similarly the last line of Frost's "Once by the Pacific" refers to the destruction of the world by saying, "Until God's last *Put out the light*' is spoken." The quoted words are a paraphrase of "Let there be light"—the words that announced the creation. In addition, we are reminded that Othello says, "Put out the light, and then put out the light" just before he strangles Desdemona. Obviously the author assumes a certain range of knowledge in the reader (or a willingness to acquire that knowledge), and some writers, such as Ezra Pound in *The Cantos*, flatter their readers by expecting knowledge of some rather obscure sources. Usually, though, the sources of allusion are fairly well known, and some are so frequently used that they would deserve study simply as sources even if they had not high interest or merit in themselves. World history, the Bible, classical mythology, and Shakespeare's works are the most important sources of allusions. Of course no one can call up all the associations required by allusions. The reader can look up items that he recognizes as allusions important to the understanding of the work at hand. He can also remind himself that as he gains experience of

---

named (Everyman; Mr. Worldly Wiseman). This kind of writing is one of the important varieties of allegory included in our definition. The trouble with this limitation of the term is that it excludes many literary works more nearly related to allegory (even of this limited kind) than to the symbolism to which they are then assigned. Another view holds that allegory is a system of symbols. Thus the term "symbol" is confused by being made to cover two quite different devices, the univalent sign, and the multivalent symbol.

Our definition of allegory stresses, first, the connection of a series of related signs into a consistent narrative. Second, the definition stresses the arbitrary way in which signs selected

both life and literature, he will be more richly nourished by everything he reads. Alertness and a good memory help.

The effect of allusion is to reinforce and illustrate the writer's point. An allusion may, like a metaphor or simile, clarify the new and unfamiliar by relating it to something already present in the reader's experience. In addition, it may underscore the similarity of man's experience in various periods of history so that when we speak of a modern gift as a Trojan horse, for example, we are reminded that deceit playing upon curiosity and covetousness has breached defenses repeatedly through history. Finally, an allusion may enlarge the implications of a work of literature by annexing to it the significance of the work alluded to. In his "Ode: Inscribed to W. H. Channing" Emerson includes these lines:

> The over-god
> Who marries Right to Might,
> Who peoples, unpeoples,—
> He who exterminates
> Races by stronger races,
> Black by white faces,—
> Knows to bring honey
> Out of the lion;
> Grafts gentlest scion
> On pirate and Turk.

---

from an artificial world or the natural one are made to stand for abstract, complex, or absent phenomena to which they may or may not be naturally related. Third, it stresses the persistently univalent quality of the signs. We might add here that allegory may or may not include overt clues to its interpretation, but that once the general scheme of allegory is discovered (usually not a difficult matter) a consistent system of one-to-one relationships can readily be established.

By contrast, our definition of symbolism implies, first, the usual discontinuity of symbols in a symbolistic work. Rarely does one encounter a "system" of symbols. Second, the definition stresses the natural relationship of the symbol to the

"Knows to bring honey/Out of the lion" alludes to a story in the fourteenth chapter of Judges in which Samson slays a lion and leaves it exposed to the sun. Returning a few days later, he finds that bees have built honeycomb in the rotting carcass. Emerson interprets this story to mean that God can produce nourishing sweetness out of corruption. Hence the evils mentioned in the preceding lines may be understood, in Emerson's optimistic philosophy, to be preludes to good—a point made clear by the Biblical allusion.

6. Myths and Archetypes

Finally, we should recognize the modern use of myth as a kind of amplified allusion. A *myth* is a narrative telling of the exploits of gods or heroes, or dramatizing a people's beliefs about such matters as the creation of the world, the nature of the universe, or the origins and destiny of a nation. In modern critical usage, "myth" is applied not only to the tales of supposedly primitive peoples, but also to contemporary systems of belief. Thus we sometimes speak of the story of Christ's conception, birth, ministry, and martryrdom as the Christian myth. Similarly, the idea that the New World is a land where men, at last exempted from the tragic history of all other nations, will realize their dreams of freedom in innocence and peace may be called the American myth. As used in the discussion of

---

complex things it symbolizes. Third, it stresses the shifting, multiple significances of the symbol. Symbolism frequently omits overt identification of the symbol with the thing or things symbolized, and it is not susceptible of a final, unambiguous interpretation.

Several other distinctions between allegory and symbolism have been attempted. It has been suggested that allegory is an intellectual maneuver designed to disguise consciously articulated "messages," whereas symbolism is the discovery in experience of inherent meanings which can be expressed or embodied in no other way. In our definition allegory too sometimes uses the process of discovery, and conversely we see

literature, the term "myth" does not imply any judgment as to the truth or falsity of the beliefs embodied in the narrative.

Poets may retell portions of the ancient myths as a basis for a vivid narrative, or they may interpret the myth, not so much to reconstruct what it meant to the society from which it arose (as an anthropologist or historian might wish to do), as to embody a meaning for his own readers. Tennyson's "Ulysses" is a dramatic monologue which develops a character portrait of the Homeric hero based not so much on Homer's version of the character as on Tennyson's version of Victorian ideals. Shelley's *Prometheus Unbound* recreates the classic myth but also contains many references to contemporary politics, science, and philosophy. A few poets, including Blake and Yeats, have developed private mythologies, but most poets draw upon the public resources of world literature.

A retrospective view of world literature shows the frequent recurrence from the earliest times to the present of a number of themes, situations, narratives, and character types, usually rendered through dramatic symbols drawn from the author's own time. These repeated motifs are known as *archetypes*. C. G. Jung and his followers have offered the theory that archetypes recur to writers (and readers) over many generations because they embody ancient experiences of the race which survive in the racial

---

no reason to suppose that symbols are not sometimes consciously invented. Again, it has been suggested that whereas allegory uses an invented world to comment on the actual one, symbolism penetrates the opaque actual world to reveal glimpses into a transcendent ideal reality beyond the ordinary reach of the senses in the actual, phenomenal world. This suggestion assumes that only authors holding to the philosophy of metaphysical idealism could or would write symbolistic works, or that attempts at such works by materialists would be false and degenerate. In fact many writers who are not philosophic idealists write works which would have to be covered by any reasonable definition of symbolism.

memory or the collective unconscious. Opponents of this concept of an eternal underground oversoul do not deny the recurrence of archetypes or the strong emotional appeal they have to many readers; they explain the recurrence as part of a consciously transmitted cultural tradition. Prominent archetypes include, among others, the descent into Hades, the night journey, the search for a father, dying and rebirth, initiation, the Oedipus complex, woman as earth goddess, the Satan-rebel figure, and the guilty wanderer telling his tale as expiation. Maud Bodkin points out in *Archetypal Patterns in Poetry* that the death-rebirth theme is common to Dante's *Divine Comedy*, Coleridge's "The Rime of the Ancient Mariner," T. S. Eliot's "The Waste Land," and many shorter poems. In "The Rime of the Ancient Mariner" this theme merges with those of the night journey, the guilty wanderer, and the relation of heaven and hell. Identification of an archetype permits the reader to recognize the total pattern of a poem so that many otherwise obscure details become meaningful. One caution is needed: In dealing with archetypes, as with myths and allusions, we must not assume that every recurrence of a familiar element will be just like every other, but must recognize the distinctive quality contributed to tradition by each new poet.

What we have said in these pages may look like a systematic formula for dealing with a poem. We hope, rather, that the suggestions made here will help you get started. Only your own skillful reading will permit you to gain insight, and consequently enjoyment, from poems that might otherwise elude you. No set of hints, no formula, is a substitute for your own experience with poetry. Some poems will speak to you at once with a clear and insistent voice; others will keep silent for a long time. The most important thing you can do is to read and listen. Trust the poet, but trust yourself, too.

For Further Reading

W. J. COURTHOPE. *A History of English Poetry*, 6 vols. London: Macmillan & Co., 1895–1910.

GEORGE SAINTSBURY. *A History of English Prosody*, 3 vols. London: Macmillan & Co., 1906–1910.

DOUGLAS BUSH. *Mythology and the Renaissance Tradition in English Poetry*. London: Oxford University Press, 1932. New revised edition, New York: W. W. Norton & Co., 1963. Norton Library, N-187.

F. R. LEAVIS. *New Bearings in English Poetry*. London: Chatto and Windus, 1932. New edition, New York: G. W. Stewart, 1950. Ann Arbor Paperbacks, AA-36.

ELIZABETH DREW. *Discovering Poetry*. New York: W. W. Norton & Co., 1933. Norton Library, N-110.

MAUD BODKIN. *Archetypal Patterns in Poetry*. London: Oxford University Press, 1934. Oxford Paperbacks, No. 66.

DOUGLAS BUSH. *Mythology and the Romantic Tradition in English Poetry*. Cambridge, Mass.: Harvard University Press, 1937. Norton Library, N-186.

CLEANTH BROOKS and ROBERT PENN WARREN. *Understanding Poetry*. New York: Henry Holt & Co., 1938, 1950, 1960.

MAX EASTMAN. *Enjoyment of Poetry*. New and enlarged edition, New York: Charles Scribner's Sons, 1939.

JOHN CROWE RANSOM. *The World's Body*. New York: Charles Scribner's Sons, 1938.

HORACE GREGORY and MARYA ZATURENSKA. *A History of American Poetry: 1900–1940*. New York: Harcourt, Brace & Co., 1946.

DONALD A. STAUFFER. *The Nature of Poetry*. New York: W. W. Norton & Co., 1946. Norton Library, N-167.

CLEANTH BROOKS. *The Well-Wrought Urn*. New York: Harcourt, Brace & Co., 1947. Harvest Books, HB-11.

RANDALL JARRELL. *Poetry and the Age*. New York: Alfred A. Knopf, 1953. Vintage Books, K-12.

M. L. ROSENTHAL and A. J. M. SMITH. *Exploring Poetry*. New York: The Macmillan Company, 1955.

MURRAY KRIEGER. *The New Apologists for Poetry*. Minneapolis: University of Minnesota Press, 1956. Midland Books, MB-49.

JOSEPH M. KUNTZ. *Poetry Explication: A Checklist of Interpretation Since 1925 of British and American Poems Past and Present*. Revised edition, Denver: Alan Swallow, 1962. Swallow Paperbook Edition.

KARL SHAPIRO and ROBERT BEUM. *A Prosody Handbook*. New York: Harper & Row, 1965.

Index